The House That God Builds

A Manual for Christian Parenting

By Skip Heitzig

Unless the Lord builds the house,
they labor in vain who build it...
Psalm 127:1

CONNECTION
COMMUNICATIONS

Published by
CONNECTION COMMUNICATIONS
4001 Osuna Road N.E.
Albuquerque, NM 87109
1.800.922.1888
Printed in USA

Table of Contents

ACKNOWLEDGEMENTS

I am grateful for the many people who have helped me bring this project to its completed form. Discussions with teams of teachers and pastors have been very fruitful and helped to forge the direction of this biblical manual. Special thanks to Krysti Hall for her competent editing of this manuscript, arranging its content, and help in digging out the right attribution information. She did much of the work afterwards that I should have done at the beginning. Thanks, Krysti, for your diligence. Kathryn Kuhlmann helped in the early stages of this project when it was still in its seminal form. Her passion and devotion to see God honored in this curriculum inspired us to put it all together. Thanks, Kathy, for your insistence on biblical principles. Also, I appreciate Tracey McMahan for her thoroughness in sifting through the maze of my materials, which included listening to tapes and transcribing them into written form. It's not an easy task to listen to me for hours and condense the material for editing. Also my gratitude goes to my assistant, David Row, for his keen and attentive oversight on this project. Dave, you're a great parent and a great friend. Of course, the ultimate gratitude goes to God, the Father of our Lord Jesus Christ (2 Cor. 1:3) for His clear Word to guide every parent of every generation.

PREFACE
By Skip Heitzig

Relax! You heard it right—relax! Every first-time parent gets a bit uptight about being able to pull off the job of parenting successfully. When our son was born, I was both excited by the prospect of being a new dad and, at the same time, I was sobered by the weight of responsibility that I knew was coming. I wanted to be the *perfect parent*—a task that I have fallen exceedingly short of on too many occasions. There is no perfect parent in this world except One and that is God Himself (Psalm 18:30). I have discovered a bit of freedom realizing that God doesn't expect me to achieve flawlessness!

Though you can't be a perfect parent, you can be a good one, you can be a loving one, and you can be a successful one. The principles found in Scripture will help you to become all of these, and these principles form the foundation of the manual that you are holding. The Biblical approach to parenting is far superior to any other and will never be subject to the failure of the changing trends in our culture. Solomon, the son of King David, saw nations and families of many kinds and remarked, "Unless the LORD builds the house, they labor in vain who build it…" (Psalm 127:1). When you have a firm grasp of the biblical values for nurturing a family, you'll notice something happening—you'll find yourself relaxing a bit more and enjoying the process of parenting a bit more. You will have a level of confidence in your role as a parent, a confidence that comes from understanding your place in the home and that the power of God is available for you to function in that place.

That's why this book was written. Over the years I've noticed that whenever I have taught about parenting from the pulpit, or we've aired messages about the family on our radio broadcast, *The Connection*, the response was huge. We had evidently hit a hot button that people resonated with. Many would call in and request tapes and other literature regarding a healthy family and child rearing. It was obvious that people were tired of pop-psychology and legalistic methodologies that both confused and often demoralized them. It was also obvious that many wanted to find out what *God* had to say about marriage, the family, and about parenting roles. And no wonder—these were *His* inventions, not ours. Since God designed these wonderful institutions, He knows best how to make them operate at peak levels.

When you became a parent, you stepped onto a whole new path of life. It was and is a path of investing yourself into the life of another. You have stepped into the role of guide, mentor, and personality cultivator. You have become a shaper of a child's future, a template of a child's outlook, and an example of a child's entire life. Both by precept and by practice, you will be molding a very distinct personality. You will be planting your influence in the tender soil of your child's heart. You will help him respond to life's challenges. You will teach her ideas, values, and world views. You will show your child how to navigate through life, make choices, and live with the consequences of those choices. Then you will launch that child-turned-adult into the world and watch the outcome of those formative years of training. It all sounds daunting, doesn't it? It is a solemn task, but it need not be overwhelming. With a huge dose of God's grace to learn (even from some of the many mistakes we will make) and a desire to love your children as God loves us, you'll be just fine. So, relax and enjoy the wonderful and mysterious process of being a parent as you let your home become the *house that God built!*

Training Your Children

INTRODUCTION BY CHUCK SMITH

TO TRAIN...OR NOT TO TRAIN

To attain value in life, a child must be trained. Proverbs 22:6 says, "Train up a child in the way he should go, and when he is old he will not depart from it." Proverbs also tells us "...a child left to himself brings shame to his mother" (Prov. 29:15). These verses clearly tell us two things: every child needs training and the presence, absence, and effectiveness of childhood training yields long-term results.

Begin with the End in Mind

Just about any book or seminar on effectiveness will tell you setting a goal is the first step toward getting where you want to go. To train our children well, we must know the goal for which we are aiming.

Toward what goal are you training your young son? Is your highest priority making sure he gets a good education, then obtains a good job, and becomes successful in the business world? Is your aim for your daughter fixed on helping her grow into a beautiful, well-educated woman with a good career and/or a homemaker with a good marriage?

Here's my real question to you: If these are your only goals for your children, what separates you as a parent from your secular peers? Speaking to His disciples about material things, Jesus said, "For after all these things the Gentiles seek...But seek first the kingdom of God and His righteousness, and all these things shall be added to you" (Matt. 6:32-33).

Jesus also asked His disciples, "For what will it profit a man if he gains the whole world, and loses his own soul?" (Mark 8:36). Put another way, "What will it profit (my child) if he gains the whole world, and loses his own soul?"

If I don't meet my children in heaven, I will feel my life was a failure. My strongest desire for my children is that they know the Lord Jesus Christ and make Him Lord of their lives. I can't emphasize enough the importance of making that the central pillar in training our children.

God has entrusted each of us as parents with a young soul to steer toward Him. Our primary goal in training our children should be that they give their lives to Jesus Christ and grow up in relationship with Him. Relationship with Jesus Christ is literally infinitely more important than success in marriage or business.

Our model as parents is God's relationship with us as our heavenly Father. Throughout His Word, He emphasizes not doing, but *being* who He created us to be with Christ in us. In the same way, we should be far more interested in who our children are, and are becoming, as children of God, than what they accomplish in the eyes of the world.

Walk Your Walk

In addition to having a goal, training a child requires personal discipline. Just as we strive to model our own lives after the character of our heavenly Father, our children look to us as their role models. They watch everything we do and copy us at every opportunity.

They learn about being parents from the way we treat them. They develop perceptions of the roles of husband and wife by how their parents treat each other. Our children learn from us how to be an adult, spouse, parent, and follower of Jesus Christ. How we behave and who we are have much more influence on our children's development than anything we say about behavior.

When I was in second grade, a man came to visit us. He arrived in a chauffeur-driven Pierce Arrow, and I can still remember the excitement of seeing the chauffeur open the door and the gentleman getting out and coming into our house. After kissing all of us, he said to the kids: "Never smoke; it's a horrible habit. I'll give you gold watches on your twenty-first birthday if you never smoke." When he left, I remember saying to my mom, "How come he told us never to smoke when he was smoking the whole time he was here?" Kids pick up on hypocrisy. What we do impacts our children far more than what we say.

Here's a fact that makes many parents uncomfortable: We can't train our children to be better people than we are. Our children naturally do what they see us doing. In some cases, they may receive training from others—teachers, coaches, pastors, mentors, friends' parents, etc.—that helps mold their behavior and character in ways that exceed our own weaknesses. Nonetheless, God's plan is for us as parents to assume primary responsibility for our children's spiritual training. This is why, when we dedicate children to God, we almost always pray for the parents. Parents cannot give to their children what they don't have themselves.

Mount a Strong Defense

Remember two things each time you look into the face of a little child. First, "Foolishness is bound up in the heart of a child…" (Prov. 22:15). Second, Jesus loves that child so much that He died on the cross to redeem that child from the power of sin. Two opposing forces are vying for the control of that child's life: the power of the Holy Spirit and the forces of darkness and evil.

As we train our children, we must ask God to help us build a strong offense and a strong defense. We must guard against and drive back the forces that tempt our children to disobey and lie. As we combat these, we need to look for opportunities to lead our children toward Jesus Christ.

One defense is to ensure, for as long as we can, that our children's lives are filled with influences that encourage development of their spiritual character rather than human nature. Pay attention to the lyrics of the music your child listens to and the television and movies your child watches; these have a tremendous effect upon shaping a child's ideas and character.

"Foolishness is bound up in the heart of a child." When children see foolishness, they're attracted to it. Part of "training up a child in the way he should go" is surrounding him with the right influences. God help our children and God help the world if we allow media to become the major influence in their development.

Two opposing forces are vying for the control of that child's life: the power of the Holy Spirit and the forces of darkness and evil.

Know Your Child

Training a child involves recognizing certain facts about that child. In some Bible translations, Proverbs 22:6 tells us to train a child according to "his way." Each child has a different "way"—a unique temperament and personality. To train our children effectively, and for our children to feel we understand and respect them for who they are, we need to be aware of each child's temperament.

Some children lack self-confidence. Encourage them. Praise them for the good work they do and the good things about their character. Tell them often how much you love them and what you appreciate about them.

Other children feel they can do anything. They barely have to study, perform well without practicing, and pick up new skills at the drop of a hat. You have to hold the reins on those children. One of our little daughters used to say, "I can do anything. I can paint. I can do ballet. I can sing opera. I can do anything." We had to constantly hold her back. Conversely, one of our sons needed all the encouragement we could give.

How would each of your children react if you were to comment "Oh, you're crazy"? One child might laugh while another might become depressed for a week. To effectively train each child according to "his way," we must recognize each child's temperament and relate to him or her accordingly.

Profound Responsibility: Precious Promise

The whole text of Proverbs 22:6 reads, "Train up a child in the way he should go, and when he is old he will not depart from it." God created us to return to our roots. You may experience conflict during the teen years when your children are seeking to discover who they are and where they fit in. However, God promises that if your children have received proper training, they will eventually return to "the way they should go."

I'll conclude by reemphasizing something I addressed earlier. One of the greatest things children need to see in their parents is consistency. If your children hear you sing about the wonderful peace Jesus gives, yet they see you repeatedly worry and become upset, they'll begin to question Jesus' peace. Likewise, if you teach your children the importance of honesty and then dishonestly take advantage of someone, they'll believe telling a lie can be better than telling the truth. Consistency is essential, whether or not you think your children are watching or listening.

Parents, you have been entrusted by God with a profound responsibility: "Train up a child in the way he should go." You have also been given a precious promise: "When he is old, he will not depart from it."

THE *Christian Home*

GOD'S TRAINING GROUND

THE BATTLEFIELD

Two main trends are shaping society's view of families today. The first is that family is "in." Family films are "Hollywood's hot tickets," says the *New York Times*.[1] A focus on family time has increased demand for board games.[2] "Family values," "quality time," and "work/life balance" are phrases heard with frequency in diverse settings: at the office, in the gym, on the golf course, and in the schools. To retain top talent and more well-balanced workers, many Fortune 500 companies offer flexible schedules, work-from-home options, and a bevy of benefits to help balance non-work responsibilities in order to create more family time when not at work.[3] Family themes are increasingly reflected in books, television, and even rap music.[4]

Paralleling this surge of interest in family is the deterioration of the real family. No matter where we look in modern society, we see division and rebellion—both in the body of Christ and in the world. Seemingly, war has been declared on marriage and whole families. One author writes, "The best thing the human society could do is to abolish the family altogether. The family is the primary conditioning device for a Western imperialistic worldview."[5] The very thing God instituted, this writer says should be abolished.

The idea of women and men forfeiting their identity as individuals and coming together as one flesh is seen by many as medieval stupidity. Becoming a full-time wife and mother is often considered a worthless investment. Families are breaking up; half of all marriages end in divorce. Just twenty-seven percent of American kids live with both their biological mother and father.[6] Children and youth are rebelling against their parents and other authorities.

BUILDER'S NOTES

Why are families falling apart during a time when family is in the spotlight? We've tried education and laws with little or no results. All the books, magazines, and movies emphasizing the family have left out the key ingredient for family success: God's wisdom.

In a recent Gallup poll, respondents identified "ethics/moral/family decline/children not raised right" as the second most important problem facing the United States.[7] A recent *USA Today* article entitled "Is the U.S. Morally in Trouble?" had this to say about American families:

> The good news is that the vital role of the traditional family at long last is the subject of national attention. The breakdown of the family… is widely recognized now as the real root cause of rising rates of substance abuse, teen suicide, abortion, academic failure, welfare dependency, and violent crime.

> The bad news, though, is that this time bomb isn't ticking—it already has exploded, and we are experiencing the fallout. Nearly one-third of all children are now born to single mothers. If this trend continues, in twenty years, nearly half of all children in our nation will be born out of wedlock.

> Our children need capable, responsible parents who have made a lifelong commitment to each other within the specific institution of marriage. This is because children need stability and consistency in their lives. They need the thousands of little moral and practical lessons that are taught in the context of daily family life. Above all, they need the love that only a mother and father can give.[8]

Another article summarizes today's youth this way:

> Born in the late 1970s and early 1980s, today's college freshmen… do not know…what it is like to live in a society in which marriage is the predominant social institution. They do, however, know about broken homes and single-parent families, as well as what it is like to be the children of child care, because 67 percent of them have mothers working outside their homes.[9]

Why are families falling apart during a time when family is in the spotlight? We've tried education and laws with little or no results. All the books, magazines, and movies emphasizing the family have left out the key ingredient for family success: God's wisdom. They've dismissed the One who created the institution of family and tried to create their own wisdom about marriages and "alternative" families. Psychologists and celebrities are redefining the family and roles of husband, wife, parent, and child…and it's not working. The author of one of the preceding articles continues: "Although millions of us still attend church and profess to believe in a Creator, we hold ourselves aloof from God. He is not, as He should be, the most important, guiding force in our daily lives."[10]

God's solution is a new heart, not just a reform program or new laws. Christians—Christian husbands, wives, parents, and children—ought to be different. People should be able to see Jesus Christ in our lives. We ought to be different husbands and wives with different marriages and different families than the world. What grieves me more than pornography, violent crime, or any of the other evils that plague our society, is seeing compromise and lack of commitment in the church of Jesus Christ today. Too often, I find Christians attempting to justify their struggles at home by comparing their families to those of unbelievers. If we feel the need to compare, we need to compare to the baseline given to us in God's Word.

THE TRAINING

Howard Hendricks said profoundly, "If your Christianity doesn't work at home, it doesn't work. Don't export it!"[11]

God calls every Christian to serve Him in some capacity, whether in a secular job, full-time ministry, at work, or at play. Each day we live, we are part of a real battle for real lives on a real battlefield with eternal consequences. To equip us to fight to the best of our ability, God tells us in His Word that basic training must begin in the home. This is where we learn to be soldiers, learn about the battle, and are molded for service as Christians. Children are soldiers in training. Parents are God's partners in training them.

First Things First

Scripture is filled with wisdom, instruction, and examples of God's design for the Christian home, and family, much of which we'll read about and discuss throughout this workbook.

We find some of the most concise instructions in Paul's writings to the Colossians and Ephesians. In both of these letters we see a pattern consistent throughout Paul's writings: He begins by addressing his most important point in general terms, and then moves to the practical level with instructions for living and growing.

Christ

Paul begins his letter to the Colossians by writing about Jesus—the head of the church and "firstborn over all creation":

> *He is the image of the invisible God, the firstborn over all creation. For by Him all things were created that are in heaven and that are on earth, visible and invisible, whether thrones or dominions or principalities or powers. All things were created through Him and for Him. And He is before all things, and in Him all things consist. And He is the head of the body, the church, who is the beginning, the firstborn from the dead, that in all things He may have the preeminence. Col. 1:15-18*

BUILDER'S NOTES

Howard Hendricks said profoundly, "If your Christianity doesn't work at home, it doesn't work. Don't export it!"

Similarly, he tells the Ephesians:

> *...according to the working of [God's] mighty power which He worked in Christ when He raised Him from the dead and seated Him at His right hand in the heavenly places, far above all principality and power and might and dominion, and every name that is named, not only in this age but also in that which is to come. And He put all things under His feet, and gave Him to be head over all things to the church, which is His body, the fullness of Him who fills all in all.* Eph. 1:19-23

> *Jesus Christ Himself being the chief cornerstone, in whom the whole building, being fitted together, grows into a holy temple in the Lord, in whom you also are being built together for a dwelling place of God in the Spirit.* Eph. 2:20-22

The Christian

Once he has reminded us of the preeminence and sovereignty of Jesus, Paul begins to discuss how Jesus' identity, actions, and position affect every area of our lives. First, Jesus saved our lives and forgave our sins:

> *And you, being dead in your trespasses...He has made alive together with Him, having forgiven you all trespasses, having wiped out the handwriting of requirements that was against us, which was contrary to us. And He has taken it out of the way, having nailed it to the cross.* Col. 2:13-14

Next, Jesus, Lord of the universe, wants to be Lord of our lives. In the first part of Colossians chapter 3, Paul discusses the importance of putting off old sinful behaviors and putting on the "new man who is renewed in knowledge according to the image of Him who created him" (Col. 3:10). In his letter to the Ephesians, he addresses marriage in greater detail:

> *Wives, submit to your own husbands, as to the Lord. For the husband is head of the wife, as also Christ is head of the church; and He is the Savior of the body. Therefore, just as the church is subject to Christ, so let the wives be to their own husbands in everything. Husbands, love your wives, just as Christ also loved the church and gave Himself for her, that He might sanctify and cleanse her with the washing of water by the word, that He might present her to Himself a glorious church, not having spot or wrinkle or any such thing, but that she should be holy and without blemish. So husbands ought to love their own wives as their own bodies; he who loves his wife loves himself. For no one ever hated his own flesh, but nourishes and cherishes it, just as the Lord does the church. For we are members of His body, of His flesh and of His bones. "For this reason a man shall leave his father and mother and be joined to his wife, and the two shall become one flesh." This is a great mystery, but I speak concerning Christ and the church.*

Nevertheless let each one of you in particular so love his own wife as himself, and let the wife see that she respects her husband. Eph. 5:22-33

The Christian Marriage

Following his discussion of Christian character, Paul addresses the Christian marriage. "Wives, submit to your own husbands, as is fitting in the Lord. Husbands, love your wives and do not be bitter toward them" (Col. 3:18-19).

Many try to tamper with the institution of marriage. They tear apart what God has made "one flesh," and then wonder why their relationships seem like hell on earth. Here's something to keep in mind: we are creatures; He is the Creator. As mere creations of the Sovereign Creator, we have neither the right nor the capacity to tamper with a God-created institution. God first established relationship between Himself and man, then between man and his wife.[12] This has been God's pattern and priority since the beginning.

Do you want your marriage to work? Follow the instruction manual provided by the Creator of your life and of marriage itself. If you want your life to start being fulfilled, bring it in line with the purpose for which God created it. When we submit to the purpose and instructions we find in God's Word, our lives and our relationships work the way God intended.

The Christian Home

Paul continues his instructions to family members: "Children, obey your parents in the Lord, for this is right. 'Honor your father and mother,' which is the first commandment with promise: 'that it may be well with you and you may live long on the earth.' And you, fathers, do not provoke your children to wrath, but bring them up in the training and admonition of the Lord" (Eph. 6:1-4).

Notice Paul's instructions have all been short, powerful admonitions. They flow out of his previous teaching in logical sequence. First he instructs the Christian, then wives, husbands, children, and fathers. He goes on to discuss employer-employee relationships, but he mentions family relationships first. With this progression, Paul tells us the home is the first and most important place in which our Christian attributes and actions should be developed and lived out. Christ wants to be Lord of the Christian home—from the kitchen and bedroom to relationships between husband and wife and parents and children.

I'll close this section with one more quote: "There is a difference between holding beliefs and being valiant in defending beliefs."[13] As Christians, we need to combat the world's messages by valiantly defending our belief in God's design for marriage and family as described in His Word. The Holy Bible is filled with wisdom that works—not pop psychology crafted to appeal to today's society.

BUILDER'S NOTES

Do you want your marriage to work? Follow the instruction manual provided by the Creator of your life and of marriage itself. When we submit to the purpose and instructions we find in God's Word, our lives and our relationships work the way God intended.

Questions to Consider

1. What do we mean when we call Jesus Christ "Lord"? One definition of "Lord" is "the one to whom a person belongs; the master."[14] Is Jesus Christ truly Lord of your life? Is He Master over your relationships with others? In a concordance, look up the word "Lord." Write below three Scriptures that describe Jesus as Lord.

   _____

   _____

   _____

2. Read Colossians 3:18-21. When it comes to family relationships, God has something to say about each member's role. He sets the standard for the Christian home. Based on these verses, complete the following sentences:

   Wives:_____

   Husbands:_____

   Children: _____

   Fathers: _____

3. When something is broken and needs to be fixed, we can:

   ❑ Take it to the manufacturer,

   ❑ Read the owner's manual to determine how it ought to work, or

   ❑ Ignore the manufacturer and the manual and attempt to fix it on our own.

4. When something is broken in your relationship with your spouse, do you:

   ❑ Take it to the Manufacturer (God) in prayer,

   ❑ Consult the Owner's Manual (the Bible), or

   ❑ Blindly try to "fix" it on your own?

5. This chapter includes a quote from a book entitled *The Death of the Family*. Do you feel your own family is "dying"? What can you do to revive your family and help ensure its strength?

   S _____(Eph. 5:21)

   T _____(Deut. 6:6-7)

   R _____(Jas. 4:7)

   O _____(Deut. 12:28)

   N _____(Ps. 119:93)

   G _____(2 Pet. 3:18)

6. God's wisdom is essential for success in life and within the family. What do the following Scriptures say about wisdom?

Psalm 111:10 _____

Proverbs 2:6 _____

Proverbs 11:2 _____

Proverbs 16:16 _____

1 Corinthians 1:23-24 _____

James 1:5 _____

James 3:17 _____

Husbands

LEADERS AND LOVERS

As a single man, I had a phobia of the "M" word: Marriage. When my initial relationship with Lenya, the woman who is now my wife, began moving toward commitment, I broke it off for two years. Eventually we dated again, and finally I found enough courage to ask her to marry me. I'll never forget the night I proposed. Sitting with her at her father's house, I fidgeted, fumbled, and searched for poetic words. Finally I simply asked, "Will you marry me?" No sooner had she said, "Yes, I'll marry you," than I jumped to my feet and started backpedaling. "Now, wait a minute. We can't rush into this thing. We've got to talk about this. This is serious stuff." A week after proposing, I told her, "I don't think we can get married. I think we're going to have to break it up." Thankfully, she was, and is, a patient woman.

Miraculously, our wedding day arrived. And once the ceremony was over, I remember thinking, "I'm a husband now, and I'm married to my wife for the rest of our lives."

The term *husband* comes from an ancient word that means "to cultivate; to till the ground." Jesus said, "I am the true vine, and my Father is the husbandman" (John 15:1, KJV)—one who plows and cultivates land. If you were to look up *husband* in *Merriam Webster's Collegiate® Dictionary*, you would find three definitions. The first reads simply, "a male partner in a marriage." However, the second says "manager, steward," and the third says "a frugal manager." In verb form, the term is defined as "to manage prudently and economically." Putting all this together, a husband is one who prudently cultivates, produces, and manages in relationship with his wife. In other words, a husband's relationship with his wife determines the outcome of what his family produces.

From these definitions, and from the Bible's instructions, I see the husband's major responsibilities as twofold: leadership (i.e. management and stewardship) and love (i.e. cultivation).

LEADERSHIP

Ben Franklin once said, "One good husband is worth two good wives; the scarcer things are, the more they are valued."

One of our greatest needs today is strong leadership at home from men of God who are willing to lovingly lead their wives and children. Today's husbands and fathers are under attack from almost all sides, and bear the challenging responsibility of leading their families through enemy territory each day.

Steve Farrar once said that Satan has two strategies toward the family: one, alienate a husband from his wife; and two, alienate a father from his children.[15] Neither innovative nor creative, these strategies are nonetheless timelessly effective. To neutralize an army, take its commander. To deplete a nation's morale, kill its president. To ruin a church, destroy its pastor. To devastate a family, neutralize or remove its leader. As leaders of the home, men are Satan's primary targets. Husbands and fathers, if you desire to be the spiritual leader of your home, expect to be attacked.

A Leadership Model

Thankfully, God has a strategy of His own, and He equips men with all they need to play the leadership role He has given them. In the Old Testament book of Song of Solomon, we see a beautiful model of leadership in the home: a relationship between a husband who leads with authority, wisdom, and tenderness and a wife who feels secure in and submits to that leadership.

The husband generously affirms the wife: "Behold, you are fair, my love! Behold, you are fair! You have dove's eyes" (Song 1:15). In turn, the wife responds, "Behold, you are handsome, my beloved! Yes, pleasant" (Song 1:16). He continues, "Like a lily among thorns, so is my love among the daughters" (Song 2:2). She responds, "Like an apple tree among the trees of the woods, so is my beloved among the sons. I sat down in his shade with great delight, and his fruit was sweet to my taste" (Song 2:3). Then she tells her friends, "He brought me to the banqueting house, and his banner over me was love. Sustain me with cakes of raisins, refresh me with apples, for I am lovesick" (Song 2:4-5).

Banner, in this verse, refers to a public announcement. The wife is saying her husband is willing to make public and demonstrate his love for, and commitment to, her. With this banner over her, the wife is secure in her husband's love and responds willingly to his leadership.

BUILDER'S NOTES

To neutralize an army, take its commander. To deplete a nation's morale, kill its president. To ruin a church, destroy its pastor. To devastate a family, neutralize or remove its leader.

Husbands, you compete for your wives every day. The world continually tugs at wives with attempts to woo them away from their husbands and homes. What helps them remain firmly committed to their husbands? Strong spiritual leadership. When a wife feels special to her husband and is treated with respect, she feels secure in her husband's love and gladly submits to his leadership.

BUILDER'S NOTES

4 Reasons Husbands Don't Lead Their Wives and Homes

1. Many men don't know how.

2. They refuse to take the reins of leadership.

3. Some men have tried, failed, and given up.

4. Some men have not only forfeited leadership, but they have forfeited the home.

Questions to Consider

1. Husbands, in relation to your wives, which of the following things should you be cultivating?

   ❏ My wife's relationship with the Lord

   ❏ My love and affection for my wife

   ❏ My children's respect for their mother

   ❏ All of the above

2. Wives, have you ever thought of a husband as one who cultivates or tills? What is the most important thing you would like to see cultivated in your marriage? _____

3. In Luke 8:4-15, Jesus tells a parable of a sower who went out to sow seeds. Men, according to the following Scriptures, what are some tools you might use to help "till" the soil of your family's hearts to help God's seeds sprout and bear fruit in their lives?

   Proverbs 19:22 _____

   1 Timothy 6:11 _____

   Ephesians 4:32 _____

   1 Peter 3:9 _____

4. Read Song of Solomon 1:15-16. When was the last time you complimented your mate? Write an affirmation of your spouse, then share that compliment with him or her today.

5. Read Ephesians 6:13-17. List below the armor we must put on to protect us against and help us attain victory over Satan's continual attack upon families and their leaders.

   The belt of _____ (v. 14)

   The breastplate of _____ (v. 14)

   The shoes of the _____ (v. 15)

   The shield of _____ (v. 16)

   The helmet of _____ (v. 17)

   The sword of _____ (v. 17)

Strength in Numbers

A Chinese proverb says, "It is harder to lead a family than to rule a nation." Further, I believe a man's leadership of his home is both more important and of greater impact than one person's leadership of a nation. I often hear Christians say, "We need a Christian president. If only we had a Christian in the White

House...." In response, I say, "If only we had strong spiritual leaders in our own houses...."

Satan is not alone in his attack against the home. He has partnered with the society and culture by which we're surrounded. Yet, we are neither outclassed nor overpowered. God is on our side, and we are part of a worldwide family of His children. Not one of us has to fight this battle alone.

Men, I encourage you to make a covenant today to pray for, deepen relationships with, and encourage the husbands and fathers in your life. Pray for and with these men to be strong spiritual leaders at home, to love as Christ loved, and to be committed as Christ was committed. Genuinely care for these men, and take the initiative to ask when God prompts you, "How are you and your wife really doing?"

Question to Consider
Friendships with other Christians are important for both men and women. A godly friend is one with whom you can pray, who will hold you accountable, and with whom you can share personal matters. Do you have a friend like this? Read Proverbs 18:24 and 27:17. What do these Scriptures tell us about friendship?

_____

_____

_____

Absence of Leadership
Perhaps you've heard the story of the man who died and went to heaven. The first thing he noticed was two lines, each with a sign. The sign over the first line, which stretched as far as the man could see, said, "Men who were dominated by their wives." The sign over the second line, in which stood only one man, said, "Men who were not dominated by their wives." The man who had just died approached the lone man in the second line, put his hand on his shoulder and asked, "How'd you do it? What was the secret?" The man replied, "I'm not sure I know. My wife told me to stand in this line, so here I am."

For several reasons, many husbands don't lead their wives and homes. Reason number one: Many men don't know how. They didn't receive healthy leadership from their fathers growing up, it wasn't modeled for them elsewhere, and no one taught them how to do it or that they should do it. Some men refuse to take the reins of leadership because they are unwilling to invest the energy or accept the responsibility. Third, some men have tried, failed, and given up. Perhaps, as in the illustration above, they're married to wives who refuse to recognize their husbands as God's ordained family leaders and have instead claimed the role for themselves. Last, some men have not only forfeited leadership, but they have forfeited the home. Some are unwilling to be a

BUILDER'S NOTES

A Wife's Response to Her Husband's Lack of Leadership:

1. She might detach herself from her spouse and children.

2. She might assume leadership responsibilities herself.

3. She might turn her anger and betrayal inward, where it festers into angry outbursts or destructive depression.

husband to the mother of their children or the wife with whom they exchanged vows. Some have died before their time, leaving a wife without a husband and/or children with no father.

Whether or not she knows it or acts like it, a wife is created to complement the leadership of her husband. When that leadership is missing, she responds in one of several ways. Like her husband, she might detach herself from her spouse and children, and divert her energy and attention outside the home, where she might receive greater affirmation and security from others. She might assume leadership responsibilities herself, but at the same time develop an attitude of ongoing resentment, cynicism, and distrust toward others, partnered with the belief that she must do everything herself. I'm convinced this response has generously fueled women's liberation. Third, she might turn her anger and betrayal inward, where it festers into angry outbursts or destructive depression that can ultimately lead to suicide. She might have an affair, partly to punish her husband, and partly because she is in search of the leadership missing from her marriage.

With all this in mind, it doesn't take much to imagine the damaging and lasting impact a father who fails, neglects, or refuses to assume leadership of his home has on his children. Men, I urge you to assume the position to which God has called you—that of spiritual leader of your home.

Questions to Consider

1. One of the most important things a man can do for his wife is spiritually lead his family. Men, do you exercise spiritual leadership in your home? If the answer is yes, what is the evidence that you are a spiritual leader? If the answer is no, how will you commit to begin learning how to exercise leadership *today*?

   _____

   _____

2. Briefly describe the character of your father when you were growing up.

   _____

   _____

3. Did your dad model supportive, loving leadership? If your father was not present in your home, was there another man in your life who influenced you and was a good role model? What are some of the values your father or mentor taught you?

   _____

   _____

LOVE

In addition to being a leader, a husband is to be a cultivator and nurturer. In Colossians 3:19, we find God's clear instructions to husbands: "Husbands, love your wives and do not be bitter toward them." In Ephesians, Paul gives more specific instructions:

> *Husbands, love your wives, just as Christ also loved the church and gave Himself for her, that He might sanctify and cleanse her with the washing of water by the word, that He might present her to Himself a glorious church, not having spot or wrinkle or any such thing, but that she should be holy and without blemish. So husbands ought to love their own wives as their own bodies; he who loves his wife loves himself. For no one ever hated his own flesh, but nourishes and cherishes it, just as the Lord does the church. …"For this reason a man shall leave his father and mother and be joined to his wife, and the two shall become one flesh." This is a great mystery, but I speak concerning Christ and the church. Nevertheless let each one of you in particular so love his own wife as himself.* Eph. 5:25-33

These were radical statements when Paul wrote them. In Paul's lifetime and culture, wives were commodities— pieces of property. Under both Jewish and Greek laws and customs, all the privileges belonged to the husband and all the duties to the wife.[16] Paul's words to the Ephesians and Colossians were intended to grab their attention—just as they are meant for us today.

Questions to Consider

1. By becoming "one flesh" with our spouses, we pledge or bind ourselves to them. Make some time to be alone with your spouse this week. Express your love in a heartfelt way. Renew your commitment to remain together until "death do you part" or the Lord's return. Use the space below to write your thoughts.

   _____

   _____

   _____

2. How would your children describe the love they witness between you and your spouse? Are you good role models of how godly husbands and wives ought to love each other?

   _____

   _____

   _____

⌂ BUILDER'S NOTES

Paul tells husbands to love their wives with the highest kind of love expressed in the Greek language—unconditional, irrevocable, perfect love.

Unconditional Love

"Husbands, love your wives." Many husbands would like to stop reading there. If we did, we could perhaps say, "I do! I love my wife." But the verse continues "…just as Christ also loved the church and gave Himself for her." That isn't so easy, is it? How did Christ love the church?

According to Romans 5:8, "…while we were still sinners, Christ died for us." This is how God's Word tells husbands they are to love their wives. Even if she sins, her husband must love her. John 1:11 tells us Jesus "…came to His own, and His own did not receive Him." But Jesus loved them anyway, and gave His life for them. Husbands are to love their wives selflessly with no strings attached—the way Christ expressed His love for us.

Builder's Notes

Falling in love is easy; growing in love is hard. Growing in love requires work, commitment, and loving when you don't feel like it.

Many of us have heard the Greek word Paul uses in Colossians 3:19: *agape*. Yet I'm convinced most of us don't understand its meaning, because we rarely love this way. Paul doesn't use *eros*, the Greek word for erotic love. Neither does Paul use *phileos*, the Greek term for love between friends. God knows marriage requires a stronger bond than these. Paul tells husbands to love their wives with the highest kind of love expressed in the Greek language—unconditional, irrevocable, perfect love. This is the way God loves us. He loves us as an act of His will, not just emotion. He loves us unconditionally, not just when we please Him. He loves us because we need His love, not because we deserve it.

I'm convinced that when most couples vow to love one another "for better, for worse, for richer, for poorer," they believe they'll only encounter "better" and "richer." They may still repeat the words, "till death do us part," but their actions reflect commitments closer to "till feelings do us part," "till debt do us part," or "till expectations do us part." The world loves people who possess exceptional appeal. When that appeal—appearance, ability, character, or position—fades or disappears, the world's love goes looking for a new target. Could anything more strongly indicate this than the current divorce rate?

Think back to your dating days, husbands. Remember the first time you laid eyes on your spouse? Something about her attracted you: the way she looked, her personality, her intelligence, or her smile. Something drew you to her. Then you started dating. You discovered even more qualities you liked… and you discovered some not-so-neat ones, too. Some of your enamored feelings began to fade, but overall you were still "in love." Then came the big question: "Will you marry me?" You got married. And you began learning what real love looks like.

Hopefully your relationship prior to marriage had developed deeper roots than surface attraction. While I am convinced God wants us to be attracted to each other, marriage requires a bond far stronger than initial attraction. We all lose our youth a little at a time, and wit and flexibility sometimes disappear when faced with stress and increased responsibility.

A Christian truly ready for a lifelong marriage commitment should be able to say to his or her intended spouse: "I love you and recognize there are many neat things about you. I also recognize there are some rotten things about you. My love is deep enough to love all of you. Even if those things that drew us together change, I will keep my commitment to love you for a lifetime." To experience marriage as God intended and love as Christ loved the church, couples must grow past interest, attraction, and infatuation—to develop mature love that remains unshakably committed. While attraction and emotion are part of what God wants for marriage, when things get tough, the only tie that will bind is unconditional love.

Falling in love is easy; growing in love is hard. Growing in love requires work, commitment, and loving when you don't feel like it. This kind of love completely opposes worldly love. This kind of selfless love is how Jesus loves us.

Questions to Consider

1. Agape love describes the kind of love God has for us—unconditional and irrevocable. Is your love for your spouse conditional? Is it dependent on what he or she does for you? Does it fluctuate in proportion to the way you are loved? Even if you didn't recite traditional marriage vows on your wedding day, you can probably fill in the blanks below. We are to love our spouses:

   a. For better or for _____

   b. For richer or for _____

   c. In sickness or in _____

   d. Forsaking all _____

   Until death do us part.

2. Christ loved the church unconditionally, and husbands are to love their wives in the same manner. Husbands, do you love your wife unconditionally? Do you ever withhold your love based on how she acts or looks?

   _____

   _____

3. Read Ephesians 5:22-25 and complete the following sentence: If a husband truly loves his wife as C_____ loved the c_____, she is much more likely to s_____ to her husband as to the L_____.

4. The ultimate demonstration of unconditional love was Jesus' sacrifice for us on the cross. Read Romans 5:8 and write the verse below:

   _____

   _____

Continual Love

The directive in Colossians 3:19 could perhaps be more clearly translated this way: "Husbands, love your wives continually." Keep loving them—actively, repeatedly, day after day, without interruption, without end.

The absence of continual love is the reason many marriages fail. Too often, the relationship progression between husband and wife goes like this: Before and perhaps during the first part of the marriage, the man profusely demonstrates his love for his wife. He goes all out to win her heart and convince her he's the guy she loves. Eventually, however, the newness, romance, and adventure of marriage become replaced by the routines of everyday life. A mind shift takes place. The man thinks to himself, "Why am I working so hard to create romance and specialness? I got her. We're married." He stops doing the big and little things that communicate to his wife (and remind him) how special she is to him. With the absence of effort to fuel and stoke the fire, the flame of love cools to room temperature and keeps on dropping. The standard plummets from mutual satisfaction to maintenance of the status quo.

An unknown author once said, "Getting married is easy. Staying married is more difficult. Staying happily married for a lifetime would be considered among the fine arts." This statement has seemingly been validated by the approximately 50 percent of today's marriages ending in divorce.

I keep in my files a copy of a letter James Dobson's father wrote to his fiancé about their imminent marriage. I like to read it at weddings because it illustrates the love of a man fully aware of all the marriage covenant includes and courageously willing to commit to it "to the end of our lives together."

I want you to understand and be fully aware of my feelings concerning the marriage covenant we are about to enter. I've been taught at my mother's knee and in harmony with the Word of God that marriage vows are inviolable, and by entering into them I'm binding myself absolutely and for life. The idea of estrangement from you through divorce for any reason, although God allows one— infidelity— will never at any time be permitted to enter into my thinking. I'm not naïve in this. On the contrary, I'm fully aware of the possibility, unlikely as it now appears, that mutual incompatibility or other unforeseen circumstances could result in extreme mental suffering. If such becomes the case, I am resolved for my part to accept it as a consequence of the commitment that I am

BUILDER'S NOTES

Good marriages are not automatic. Like any living thing, marriage requires attentive nurturing in order to grow and thrive.

now making, and to bear it, if necessary, to the end of our lives together. I've loved you dearly as a sweetheart, and I will continue to love you as my wife. But over and above that, I love you with a Christian love that demands I never react in any way toward you that would jeopardize our prospects of entering heaven, which is the supreme objective of both of our lives. And I pray that God himself will make our affection for one another perfect and eternal.[17]

When God gives a command, He invariably provides an example for us to follow. In this case, God's model for husbands in loving their wives is Christ's love for the church: "Husbands, love your wives, just as Christ also loved the church…" (Eph. 5:25). This verse reminds us that Christ loves us continually. He continually wants to spend time with us. He continually uses His Word, His Holy Spirit, blessings in our lives, and others around us to let us know how special we are to Him. This is the way God instructs husbands to love their wives: with uninterrupted, unwavering commitment.

God also gives us an example of what continual love does *not* look like. In His letter to the church at Ephesus, Jesus writes, "…I have this against you, that you have left your first love" (Rev. 2:4). By "first love," Christ means the espousal, courting love the church once had toward Christ. God intends this love to remain constant, if not grow in passion, rather than wane from neglect.

Good marriages are not automatic. Like any living thing, marriage requires attentive nurturing in order to grow and thrive. I believe few Christian marriages know and experience the kind of security and love God intended between husbands and wives. Husbands, love your wives continually.

Questions to Consider

1. **Then & Now:** Men, think back to the ways you demonstrated affection for your wife when you dated her before your marriage. Check in the column at the left, any of the evidences of affection that apply. Then evaluate your demonstrations of affection now. Place an X in the column that most accurately describes the consistency with which you express your affection today.

A. I told her often how much I cared for her:
- ❏ When we were dating
- ❏ I still do this today
- ❏ I need to do this more often
- ❏ I don't do this anymore

B. I frequently asked her opinion:
- ❏ When we were dating
- ❏ I still do this today
- ❏ I need to do this more often
- ❏ I don't do this anymore

BUILDER'S NOTES

Most men are taught early to sacrifice for career, so they can provide generously for their families, send their kids to college, and retire in comfort. Yet, how many men are taught to sacrifice for their wives?

C. I faithfully attended church with her:
- ❏ When we were dating
- ❏ I still do this today
- ❏ I need to do this more often
- ❏ I don't do this anymore

D. I read the Bible to her:
- ❏ When we were dating
- ❏ I still do this today
- ❏ I need to do this more often
- ❏ I don't do this anymore

E. I paid her compliments:
- ❏ When we were dating
- ❏ I still do this today
- ❏ I need to do this more often
- ❏ I don't do this anymore

F. I treated her with courtesy and respect:
- ❏ When we were dating
- ❏ I still do this today
- ❏ I need to do this more often
- ❏ I don't do this anymore

G. I agreed to spend the day doing what she wanted:
- ❏ When we were dating
- ❏ I still do this today
- ❏ I need to do this more often
- ❏ I don't do this anymore

2. The term *commit* means "obligate, bind; to pledge or assign to some particular course or use." In the following Scriptures, what are we told to commit to the Lord?

Job 5:8 _____

Psalm 31:5 _____

Psalm 37:5 _____

Proverbs 16:3 _____

3. We demonstrate our love for God by the way we love each other. Turn to 1 John 2:5 and complete the following sentences:

Whoever _____ , the love of God is _____.

1 John 2:10—He who loves his brother _____.

1 John 4:8—He who does not love, _____,
for God is love.

1 John 5:3—For this is the love of God, that we _____.

4. Love is an act, not necessarily a feeling. What do the following Scriptures
   tell us about love?

John 3:16 _____

John 13:34 _____

John 14:15 _____

John 15:13 _____

Sacrificial Love

The Gulf War reminded me of a duty that binds our nation's men. Though
most are never called to demonstrate it, each man must be willing to sacrifice
his own life for the freedoms of his family and country. God holds husbands
responsible for a similar sacrifice: "Husbands, love your wives, just as Christ also
loved the church and gave Himself for her" (Eph. 5:25). Jesus sacrificed His life
for us. Likewise, husbands are to love their wives sacrificially. In other words,
the husband's role is one of giving rather than getting.

One of the great tests of every marriage is what the husband is willing to
give up for his wife. When asked if they would die for their wives, most husbands say "yes." Why, then, do men struggle when asked to make lesser sacrifices at home—like painting the kitchen on a perfect afternoon to play golf?
A little time on the golf course is nothing compared to sacrificing your life.
Yet, dying to self is hard, isn't it?

Most men are taught early to sacrifice for career, so they can provide generously for their families, send their kids to college, and retire in comfort. Yet,
how many men are taught to sacrifice for their wives?

Paul continues: "...that He might sanctify and cleanse her with the washing
of water by the word" (Eph. 5:26). What a beautiful picture of Jesus' love for
us. Jesus loves us, forgives us, and bathes us in God's Word. As He forgives us,
He constantly reminds us that no matter how often or how severely we mess up,
He will keep on forgiving and cleansing us.

Do you see the example here for husbands? When marital conflict arises,
husbands are to initiate reconciliation, sacrifice pride, and be the first to
forgive—even if it's her fault. Especially if it's her fault. Husbands are to love
their wives as Christ loved the church. Christ doesn't make mistakes, but we
do—and He forgives us every time.

BUILDER'S NOTES

When a husband treats his wife well and expresses care and affection, he creates within her a sense of well-being and security in her husband's love.

Questions to Consider

1. Husbands, if someone asked you, "Are you willing to die for your wife?" how would you respond? Look up the word *sacrifice* in a dictionary and write its definition below.

_____

_____

_____

BLUEPRINTS 📖

"Likewise you husbands, dwell with them with understanding, giving honor to the wife, as to the weaker vessel, and as being heirs together of the grace of life, that your prayers may not be hindered."

1 Peter 3:7

2. The Bible speaks often about sacrifice. What new insights do you gain from the following Scriptures?

Romans 12:1 _____

Ephesians 5:2 _____

Hebrews 9:26 _____

Hebrews 13:15 _____

3. Consider how you utilize your time during an average week. Do you regularly spend time alone with your spouse without any distractions? If the answer is no, write down one thing you will change about your present schedule to make time for your spouse. _____

_____

4. Complete the following statement. This week I will love my wife selflessly by:

_____

_____

_____

Affectionate Love

Fourth, husbands are to love with great affection. Paul continues, "…husbands ought to love their own wives as their own bodies; he who loves his wife loves himself. For no one ever hated his own flesh, but nourishes and cherishes it, just as the Lord does the church" (Eph. 5:28-29).

Guys, think how we spoil ourselves. We get up, shave, shower, fix our hair, get dressed, and put on cologne. Why? We want to look good. We go to the kitchen, prepare a meal (or someone prepares it for us), and eat. Why? We want to stay alive. Some of us even exercise. When we do all this for our bodies, we become living examples of a basic truth: we love ourselves. This is the way Ephesians 5:28 tells husbands to love their wives.

One way we "nourish and cherish" our bodies is by investing time in them. Likewise, by spending time with his wife, a husband "nourishes and cherishes" her. Peter tells husbands, "Husbands, likewise, dwell with them with understanding, giving honor to the wife…that your prayers may not be hindered" (1 Pet. 3:7).

Husbands, how much time do you spend with your wife? I mean really spend together, nurturing the relationship. In an article entitled "Marriages Made to Last," *Psychology Today* summarized the results of a survey administered to hundreds of happily married couples. Two of the most common responses from these happy couples were: "My spouse is my best friend" and "I love and like my spouse as a person." From the survey, the researchers concluded that time together—both quality and quantity—is a key ingredient of a happy marriage.

When we treat ourselves well, we cultivate our own sense of well-being. Similarly, when a husband treats his wife well and expresses care and affection, he creates within her a sense of well-being and security in her husband's love.

Many men find taking care of their bodies far easier than verbalizing their love. Words like "I love you" and "You are special to me" get stuck in their throats. Instead, they want to point back to the marriage contract and say, "Look on the dotted line. I said I loved you twenty years ago. Believe me, all right? You've got it in writing." Perhaps this is why many marital problems occur as a result of a wife not feeling secure in her husband's love. Depending on when or whether a husband expresses care for his wife, she may feel his love is conditionally based on how she looks or behaves, expressed only when he wants something in return, or completely nonexistent.

Other husbands have put their love into words and actions, and received rejection in response. These men say with frustration, "My wife is unresponsive. Every time I try to express affection, she pulls back and gets angry." If this is you, here's my advice: Don't give up. Clobber her with your love. Win her back. Woo her tenderly. I can't guarantee her response, but I can assure you of this: Each man is responsible for his own role. God tells husbands to love their wives "just as Christ also loved the church and gave Himself for her." The church rejected Christ. Yet, Christ loved her and gave Himself for her with great affection.

BUILDER'S NOTES

There's something wrong in a marriage when the husband views his wife merely as a cook, house-cleaner, childcare worker, and sex partner.

Questions to Consider

1. Husbands, ask yourself the following question: Do I love my wife? Rank your love on a scale of 1 to 10, with 1 being "totally unloving" and 10 being "perfectly loving." _____

   Now ask yourself, Do I love my wife as Christ loved the church and gave Himself for her? Rank yourself again. Did the number change?_____

2. Complete the following statement. This week I will demonstrate my affection for my wife by:

   _____

   _____

3. How often do you tell your spouse, "I love you"? Does your spouse feel completely secure in your love? Commit to expressing your love verbally every day.

_____

_____

4. Read 1 Peter 3:7. If a husband does not dwell with his wife "with under-standing, giving honor" to her, what does the Bible say will happen?

_____

_____

Developmental Love

A husband's love for his wife should be developmental: "Husbands, love your wives, just as Christ also loved the church and gave Himself for her, that He might sanctify and cleanse her with the washing of water by the word, that He might present her to Himself a glorious church, not having spot or wrinkle or any such thing, but that she should be holy and without blemish" (Eph. 5:25-27). Jesus is committed to our growth. Following Jesus' example, husbands should be committed to spiritually nurturing their wives.

"Sanctify and cleanse" are words of caretaking, cultivation, and protection. As spiritual leader of the home, part of the husband's role is to draw his wife away from anything that would defile her, and instead draw her closer to Jesus Christ. Again, we look to Christ for our example.

When we sin, God does not coldly condemn us. Instead, He disciplines us, forgives us, and seeks to draw us away from the sin (Heb. 12:3-11; 1 John 1:9). "'Come now, and let us reason together,' says the LORD, 'Though your sins are like scarlet, they shall be as white as snow...'" (Isa. 1:18). Thus, we see a husband's role is not that of a judge who points out, "I see a problem in your spiritual life, honey." Rather, a godly husband comes alongside his wife, lovingly draws her away from sin, and plants her firmly upon the foundation of Jesus Christ.

There's something wrong in a marriage when the husband views his wife merely as a cook, housekeeper, childcare worker, and sex partner. Far more than these things, a wife is a special treasure from God, given to a husband to cultivate, nurture, and partner with throughout life. With loving care and skill-ful development, a husband can make his wife blossom.

How can a husband nurture his wife spiritually? Here's an example. I can relieve my wife periodically of her role as caretaker and mother. I can take my child or children away from the house and tell my wife, "Honey, I want you to have this next hour or so to be alone with God. Forget your to-do list. Just spend time with God. I want you to have time to grow spiritually."

Charles Lindbergh married Ann Morrow. The first man to fly solo across the Atlantic Ocean, Lindbergh became famous around the world. Like many men of fame, he could easily have become caught up in his celebrity and neglected his wife. Instead, he nurtured, developed, and enabled her to become one of America's most famous writers. She wrote this testimony to her marriage:

> To be deeply in love is, of course, a great liberating force. Ideally, both members of a couple in love free each other to new and different worlds. I was no exception to this general rule. The sheer fact of finding myself loved was unbelievable and changed my world. I was given confidence and strength and almost a new character. The man I married believed in me and what I could do and consequently I could do more than I even realized.[18]

Lindbergh flew across the Atlantic; Ann Morrow soared in feeling loved by her husband.

Questions to Consider

1. Read Ephesians 5:26. Jesus Christ cleanses and sanctifies the church by "the washing of water by the word." Husbands are commanded to do the same thing for their wives. Look up the following Scriptures. What do they say about the Word of God and its power?

   Luke 4:4 _____

   Luke 11:28 _____

   Hebrews 4:12 _____

   1 Peter 1:23 _____

2. Husbands, which of the following describe the way you treat your wife? Wives, which of the following describe the ways your husband treats you? Check all that apply.

   ❑ …as a helper comparable to me/him (Gen. 2:18)

   ❑ …as bone of my/his bones and flesh of my/his flesh (Gen. 2:23)

   ❑ …as important as my/his own body (Eph. 5:28)

   ❑ …as my/his fair love (Song 4:10)

   ❑ …as a treasure or as a good thing (Prov. 18:22)

3. Study Ephesians 5:26 in more depth. How can you incorporate this model into your marriage?

   _____

BUILDER'S NOTES

Negative attitudes and words expressed toward a wife deeply impact her sensitive spirit. These damage and may eventually destroy her security in her husband's love.

Tender Love

Let's return to Colossians one more time to read the second part of God's instructions to husbands. "Husbands, love your wives and do not be bitter toward them" (Col. 3:19). The word *bitter* originally meant pointed, like a piercing arrow. Today's definitions include "accompanied by severe pain or suffering, harshly reproachful, marked by intense animosity."

Being bitter can take the form of both attitude and action. Once bitterness becomes an attitude, it is moments away from becoming an action. Husbands, be aware of the state of your heart. Perhaps you are bitter about something completely unrelated to your wife. Nonetheless, this bitterness will likely end up being expressed toward your wife if you allow it to remain in your heart.

For some of us, a "do not" statement immediately brings two questions to mind: "Why not?" and "What should I do instead?" In answer to the first question, the Bible tells us some of the results of bitterness and harshness: "A soft answer turns away wrath, but a harsh word stirs up anger" (Prov. 15:1). "Pursue peace...and holiness...lest any root of bitterness springing up cause trouble, and by this many become defiled" (Heb. 12:14-15). "For I see that you are poisoned by bitterness..." (Acts 8:23). Most of us could do without anger, trouble, defilement, and poison in our marriages. By refraining from bitterness, husbands can guard against these in the home.

First Peter 3:7 gives another indication of why husbands should not be bitter toward their wives. "Husbands, likewise, dwell with them with understanding, giving honor to the wife, as to the weaker vessel, and as being heirs together of the grace of life, that your prayers may not be hindered." Since bitterness is not an expression of honor, we see here another result of a husband's bitterness toward his wife: hindrance of his prayers. In addition, we're told the wife is "the weaker vessel," and an heir with her husband in grace. Peter is not saying the wife is feeble or mentally inferior, but that she often has a more delicate frame and structure and should be treated with special kindness and attention.[19] Negative attitudes and words expressed toward a wife deeply impact her sensitive spirit. These damage and may eventually destroy her security in her husband's love. If these are expressed with frequency over time, she may begin to believe her husband's love is no longer unconditional.

Instead of bitter, how should husbands be toward their wives? I like the comparison Paul provides in Ephesians chapter 4: "Let all bitterness, wrath, anger, clamor, and evil speaking be put away from you, with all malice. And be kind to one another, tenderhearted, forgiving one another, even as God in Christ forgave you" (Eph. 4:31-32).

We find an example of a husband's tenderness toward his wife in 1 Samuel chapter 1. Hannah had been unable to conceive and bear children—something she passionately longed to do. In response, her husband treated her with compassion and tenderness, even though a wife who could not bear children was a social stigma in their culture. We read:

> *And whenever the time came for Elkanah to make an offering…to Hannah he would give a double portion, for he loved Hannah, although the LORD had closed her womb…So it was, year by year, when she went up to the house of the LORD…she wept and did not eat. Then Elkanah her husband said to her, "Hannah, why do you weep? Why do you not eat? And why is your heart grieved? Am I not better to you than ten sons?"* 1 Sam. 1:4-8

What a wonderful thing for a husband to say in a society that put so much emphasis on a woman's producing children and sons! Instead of rejecting, scorning, or being embarrassed by his childless wife, Elkanah told her, "It doesn't matter, Hannah. I love you. Our relationship is more important and better than ten sons." I love that Elkanah pursued Hannah in her grief. When Hannah wept and refused to eat, Elkanah could have said, "Oh, it'll pass. She's just going through some weird phase." Instead, he pursued her.

Husbands, you can make or break your wife. The power is within your hands. You can support her role as a wife and mother and be sensitive, or you can criticize, ridicule, ignore, and break her. The choice is yours.

Sadly, many men complain about their wives, and vice versa. When we do this, we are forgetting a fundamental truth: God created men and women to be together. After God had created man, He looked at him and said, "…It is not good that man should be alone; I will make him a helper comparable to him" (Gen. 2:18). Men, God gave women to us because we need help. We are to love our wives and consider them a gift from God. S

Questions to Consider

1. In a dictionary, look up the definition of the word *bitter* and write it below.

   _____

   _____

2. Are you ever bitter toward your spouse?
   ❏ Never bitter ❏ Sometimes ❏ Often ❏ Constantly

3. Take time to pray, asking the Lord to remove any "root of bitterness" that may have sprung up in your heart (Heb. 12:15). Ask Him to replace that bitterness with a wellspring of love for the spouse God has given you.

4. One way a man can treat his wife with bitterness is through his words. Fill in the blanks below to see what effects words can have.

   Proverbs 15:1 "A soft answer turns away _____, but a harsh word stirs up _____."

Proverbs 25:11 "A word fitly spoken is like _____."

Proverbs 12:25 "Anxiety in the heart of man causes depression, but a good word _____."

5. The first five minutes of each day with your spouse can set the tone for the remainder of the day. How do you typically greet your spouse in the morning? Is there room for improvement?_____

6. Husbands, do you realize you can make or break a good wife and mother? Do you ever see your wife cry? Are you sensitive and supportive? On a scale of 0 to 10, with 0 being totally insensitive and 10 being totally sensitive, how do you rank? _____

A FINAL WORD

Husbands, how do you love your wives? And how will you commit to love them throughout your marriage? Are you willing to say, "I will love my wife unconditionally, as Christ loved the church; sacrificially as Christ gave Himself for the church; and developmentally to cleanse her and make her more like Christ"?

I conclude with a surgeon's words describing a couple he observed, and a husband who unconditionally loves his wife.

I stand by the bed where a young woman lies. Her face postoperative. Her mouth twisted in palsy, clownish; a tiny twig of the facial nerve, one to the muscles of her mouth, has been severed. She will be this way from now on. The surgeon had followed with religious fervor the curve of the flesh, I promise you that. Nevertheless, to remove the tumor in her cheek, I had to cut the little nerve. Her young husband is in the room. He stands on the opposite side of the room and together they seem to dwell in the evening lamplight, isolated from me, private. "Who are they?" I ask myself—"He and this wry-mouthed person that I have made, who gaze and touch each other so generously, greedily." The young woman speaks, "Will my mouth always be like this?" she asks. "Yes, it will, because the nerve was cut." She nods and she is silent. But the young man smiles. "I like it," he says. "I think it's kind of cute." All at once I know who he is. I understand. I lower my gaze. One is not fooled in an encounter with a god. I'm mindful as he bends to kiss her crooked mouth. And I am so close that I can see how he twists his own lips to accommodate to hers and to show her that their kiss still works. I remember that the gods appeared in ancient Greece as mortals. And I hold my breath and I let the wonder in.[20]

Wives

Virtuous Helpers

In a local newspaper, I came across two poll-based lists: "The Ten Sleaziest Ways to Make a Living" and "The Ten Most Admirable Occupations." According to the list, a drug dealer makes his living the sleaziest way of all. This was followed, in order, by organized crime boss, television evangelist, prostitute, street peddler, local politician, congressman, car salesman, rock star, and insurance salesman.

Eight of the most admirable occupations were, respectively: firefighter, paramedic, farmer, pharmacist, grade school teacher, mail carrier, priest, and homemaker. I am encouraged that some people on this planet still think homemaker is a worthwhile, noble occupation.

THE IMPORTANT ROLE OF THE WIFE

First, let's look at Paul's instructions for the family in Colossians 3:18-21.

> *Wives, submit to your own husbands, as is fitting in the Lord. Husbands, love your wives and do not be bitter toward them. Children, obey your parents in all things, for this is well pleasing to the Lord. Fathers, do not provoke your children, lest they become discouraged.*

Note that Paul first addresses wives, and then husbands, children, and fathers with instructions of equal importance to all. This was radically new for the audience to whom Paul wrote this letter. The Jewish temple held divided courts: an outer court for Gentiles, an inner court for Jewish women, and a further inner court for Jewish men. Jewish women didn't dare enter the men's holier court, and most spiritual instruction was given to them through the men. Yet, Paul addresses wives directly and speaks to them first.

BUILDER'S NOTES

As Christians, we need to see wives and mothers the way Scripture portrays them—as women of virtue with a God-given calling and daunting responsibilities.

As I read this recently, I was struck by the tremendous importance of a wife's role—and the tremendous attack this role is receiving from society. Increasingly, popular culture is devaluing the role of homemaker and housewife. Though the Bible elevates the role of the woman and eliminates distinctions of superiority of men over women (see Prov. 31), the world says the role is outdated. A recent *TIME* cover story reported:

> The single woman has come into her own…An estimated four million …unmarried women are cohabiting with their lovers, and a growing number are being more open about gay relationships…More confident, more self-sufficient, and more choosy than ever, women no longer see marriage as a matter of survival and acceptance…More single women— especially those watching their biological clocks run down—are resorting to solo pregnancies, sperm donors, or adoption agencies. The birthrate…has climbed 15 percent among unmarried thirty-somethings since 1990. In [a] *TIME/CNN* poll, fully 61 percent of single women ages 18 to 49 answered "yes" when asked whether they would consider rearing a child on their own.[21]

Feminist Kate Millett writes, "The family unit must go, because it's the family that has oppressed and enslaved women."[22] My wife didn't know she was oppressed and enslaved until Kate told her!

I respect women who work as professionals. However, I want to counteract the notion that a woman is only half a woman if her full-time profession is that of wife and/or mother. As Christians, we need to see wives and mothers the way Scripture portrays them—as women of virtue with a God-given calling and daunting responsibilities.

We need to tell wives and mothers, "You're important. Your role is vital. We admire your strength to swim against the tide of public opinion. We admire your courage to spend your days and share your time and love with the crumb-crunchers of the family." Husbands need to tell their wives, "I want to support you in your role," and back up their words with action.

Question to Consider

Contrary to what some modern writers have said, the family has not oppressed and enslaved women. According to Romans 6:6, what is capable of enslaving us?_____

Praise God: as believers we have been freed from the power and penalty of sin! (Rom. 6:18)

SUBMISSION: WHAT IT DOES NOT MEAN

"Wives, submit to your own husbands, as is fitting in the Lord" (Col. 3:18). This verse and its counterpart, Ephesians 5:22, have held a negative—and wrong—connotation for years for millions of people. When I mention this verse during weddings, the expressions on the faces of the female audience change as if I personally insulted them. This is not entirely surprising, since popular culture, by and large, defines *submission* in such negative terms as inferiority, dependence,[23] and surrender.[24] To some, the word means resignation,[25] to succumb, give up,[26] cry "Uncle." This misunderstanding of biblical submission has led to abuses by husbands and wives, and damaged many marriages.

Servanthood

Let's examine what *submit* does not mean in the context in which Paul uses it. This verse does not give husbands permission to be dictators of the home or to treat their wives as servants or children. Paul uses two closely related words with very different meanings in this passage. In verse 18, he uses the Greek word *hupotasso*, which we translate as "submit." In verses 20 and 22, respectively addressing children and bondservants, Paul uses the word *hupakouo*, translated as "obey." Many husbands and wives have incorrectly substituted the second term for the first in their understanding and application of Paul's instructions in Colossians 3:18-22. God, however, intended the relationship between husbands and wives to be different from the relationship between parents and children, or employees and employers.

Inferiority

Neither is the word *submit* meant to indicate wives are inferior and husbands are superior. Spiritually, men and women are equal in God's eyes. Paul tells us in another of his letters, "…there is neither male nor female; for you are all one in Christ Jesus" (Gal. 3:28). William Hayden said "Woman is physically inferior to man, but intellectually his equal, socially his superior, morally more susceptible, and religiously more devotional."[27]

In addition to equality between men and women, God also established an order: "…the head of every man is Christ, the head of woman is man, and the head of Christ is God" (1 Cor. 11:3). Scripture also tells us Christ is equal with God: "…Christ Jesus, who, being in the form of God, did not consider it robbery to be equal with God" (Phil. 2:5b-6). Yet, Jesus also voluntarily submitted to His Father's will: "…He humbled Himself and became obedient to the point of death" (Phil. 2:8). Submitting to the Father did not make Jesus inferior; He was, is, and always will be equal with the Father. In the same way, submitting to their husbands does not change wives' equality with their husbands.

BUILDER'S NOTES

William Hayden said "Woman is physically inferior to man, but intellectually his equal, socially his superior, morally more susceptible, and religiously more devotional."

Seen but Not Heard

Lastly, this biblical command to wives to submit does not infer that husbands are always right and should thus be the exclusive decision-makers of the household. The Bible tells us in Proverbs 31 that the virtuous wife "…opens her mouth with wisdom" (Prov. 31:26) and "…she considers a field and buys it; from her profits she plants a vineyard" (Prov. 31:16). While being a submissive wife and a mother, the virtuous wife also makes dynamic choices and carries a lot of responsibility to keep the home running smoothly. Husbands, you ought to lean on your wives for help in making important choices. God equipped wives with wisdom and good ideas and put you two together to share the burden and yoke.

Questions to Consider

1. Read James 4:7. As believers, to whom are we to submit first and foremost?

   _____

2. Read Ephesians 5:21. To whom are wives to submit according to this verse? With what attitude are we to submit?

   _____

3. Based on the following Scriptures, what are wives commanded to do in addition to submitting?

   Ephesians 5:33b _____

   Titus 2:4 _____

   1 Corinthians 7:3 _____

   1 Corinthians 7:10 _____

4. Husbands, Ephesians 5:25 says, "Husbands, love your wives, just as Christ also loved the church… ." Read Matthew 20:28 and the rest of Ephesians 5:25. How does Christ love the church?

   _____

   _____

5. In God's sight, all people are created equal. Romans 2:11 says, "For there is no partiality with God." Read Galatians 3:28. Three groups of people are given equal standing in God's sight. Who are these three groups?

   J_____ and G_____

   s_____ and f_____

   m_____ and f_____

6. What do these Scriptures say about how God views you and your spouse?

_____

7. Examine the decision-making process in your home. Who makes most of the important decisions that affect your family?
☐ The husband   ☐ The wife   ☐ We make them together as a couple

8. Men, how often is your wife the one who makes important decisions?
☐ Never   ☐ Seldom   ☐ Occasionally   ☐ Frequently   ☐ Always

SUBMISSION: WHAT DOES IT MEAN?

Voluntary Completion

As mentioned earlier, the Greek word used for submission is *hupotasso*. This is originally a military term that means "to arrange or rank under." Most of us are familiar with the military's system of ranking: privates, sergeants, colonels, generals, etc. While each rank represents a different level and type of professional skill, the individuals who fill those ranks are of equal worth as persons. In addition, the functions performed by each rank are complementary to the others and synergistic to the whole. The word also indicates an action performed willingly and voluntarily, not by constraint. Thus, one definition of the term *submit* as used in Colossians 3:18 might be "to voluntarily complete, to adapt, to blend so as to make a complete whole, or a complete pattern."

Support

The word *hupotasso* conveys the idea of placing oneself under the authority of another, assuming responsibility and carrying a burden.[28] Sound familiar? I'm immediately reminded of Genesis 2:18: "And the LORD God said, 'It is not good that man should be alone; I will make him a helper comparable to him.'"

First, God created animals and brought them to Adam for naming. "…But," the Bible says, "for Adam there was not found a helper comparable to him" (Gen. 2:20). So God created a woman from one of Adam's ribs and brought her to Adam. Thus, Scripture tells us, a precedent was set: "Therefore a man shall leave his father and mother and be joined to his wife, and they shall become one flesh" (Gen. 2:24). God has given woman the unique position of being to man what nothing else could be—becoming one flesh with man, and making man what he could never be by himself.

I like the story of an exchange between Pete Flaherty, county commissioner in Pittsburgh, Pennsylvania, and his wife, Nancy. One day, as they were both surveying a building project in town, one of the construction workers called out,

"Nancy, remember me? We used to date in high school." Later, Pete kidded his wife, "Aren't you glad you didn't marry that guy? Today you'd be the wife of a construction worker." Without missing a beat, she responded, "No, I wouldn't. If I had married him, he'd be the county commissioner."

Enhancement

When women accept the title of "wife," they accept the job God created for them: making their husbands the best they can be. The husband's job is to lead the home and family; the wife's role is to enable him to lead to the best of his ability. One of the best ways for women to do this, God tells us, is to "submit to your own husbands, as is fitting in the Lord."

Wives, are you making it easier or more difficult for your husband to function as head of the family? Many wives answer this question with the complaint, "My husband doesn't take leadership." Unfortunately, many men fail to assume spiritual leadership or any kind of decision-making headship in the home. However, my question to the wives is, "Are you letting him?"

In the book *Staying Close*, Christian author Barbara Rainey writes a section entitled, "Thoughts for the Wife Whose Husband Won't Lead." She writes:

> One, analyze the situation objectively. Has your husband really abdicated total leadership? See if you can find some areas where he's leading and begin to appreciate and thank him for those areas. Two, be sure that you are a good follower. Some women are stronger leaders than their husbands, so he may never have had the chance to truly lead. Do a study from the Scripture on what a good follower does. Three, don't expect your husband to be the perfect leader immediately. It may take him years. And some wives are thinking, "More like millennium." But it might take him years to develop good leadership in certain areas. Give him room to grow. Four, learn to appreciate the differences between you and your husband and accept them. It may be that God has made you different in your leadership abilities and styles so that you really do need one another. And finally, pray. One of the fiercest battlegrounds today is for male leadership in the family. Your prayers could become the catalyst that unites your mate's heart to become God's man, husband, and father.[29]

Resistance of Sin

In the Garden of Eden, Adam and Eve were tempted by Satan and sinned against God. In response to that sin, God gave Eve a message that would be true for all women, "...I will greatly multiply your sorrow and your conception; in pain you shall bring forth children; your desire shall be for your husband, and he shall rule over you" (Gen. 3:16).

"Your desire shall be for your husband, and he shall rule over you." Some

---

BUILDER'S NOTES

When women accept the title of "wife," they accept the job God created for them: making their husbands the best they can be.

have interpreted the word *desire* in this verse as sexual desire. Others see it as psychological, emotional desire. However, Eve had these desires for her husband before the fall. To determine what the word means in this context, we look at other places in Scripture where the same Hebrew word was used. We find it in Genesis 4. God said to Cain, "…sin lies at the door. And its desire is for you, but you should rule over it" (Gen. 4:7). The word *desire* here is the same Hebrew word spoken to Eve in Genesis 3:16. The word means "control."

Part of the curse sin brought upon us is woman's desire to usurp man's authority, and man's unbiblical desire to put her under his feet. The battle of the sexes began with man's fall: "Your desire shall be for your husband"—feminism; "and he shall rule over you"—chauvinism. In Hebrew, the latter refers to a dictatorial, authoritarianism, unbiblical style of leadership.

As a result of sin, men and women strive against one another. However, when we accept Christ and are born again into God's family, each of us becomes a "…new man [or woman] who is renewed in knowledge according to the image of Him who created him" (Col. 3:10). God gives us the grace and strength to put off our sinful behaviors—those we received through the curse of the fall—and instead put on "…tender mercies, kindness, humility, meekness, longsuffering; bearing with one another, and forgiving one another…" (Col. 3:12-13). Through these new behaviors, relationships start to be what God intended them to become.

It takes a big dose of God's grace for a wife to say, "I willingly submit myself to you to make you all God wants you to become, and to make us as one flesh, all that God wants us to become." Similarly, it takes God's grace for a husband to say, "I love you unconditionally. I will remain at your side forever."

Responsibility

One of the biggest problems between husband and wife is something I call "role reminding." Each spouse memorizes the other's role and takes the liberty of reminding the other of his or her role. For instance, wives remind their husbands, "You're supposed to love me as Christ loved the church." Husbands remind their wives, "You're supposed to submit."

Then comes the if/then game we play with God and anyone who challenges our behavior. Husbands: "I know that the Bible says I'm to love her as Christ loved the church, but if she'd submit for once, it'd be easier to love her." Wives: "I know I'm supposed to submit as unto the Lord, but if he'd truly love me I could trust him enough to submit."

When marriage becomes more about rights, rationalizations, and blame than love for and responsibility to God and each other, it starts to fall apart. Relationships work as God intended them to when each person takes responsibility for his or her God-given role and fills it to the best of his or her ability. Even though marriage joins husbands and wives as one flesh, God does not hold

BUILDER'S NOTES

When marriage becomes more about rights, rationalizations, and blame than love for and responsibility to God and each other, it starts to fall apart.

one responsible for the behavior of the other. He does, however, hold each of us responsible for our own behavior and obedience of the instructions He gives in His Word.

Questions to Consider

1. Wives, God gave you a privilege when He appointed you as helpers to your husbands, to come alongside them and complete them. Are you making it easier or harder for your husband to function as head of your family? Check the answer below that most closely matches the way you are filling your role as a wife.

   ❑ I continually make it difficult for my husband to function as head of our family.

   ❑ I often make it difficult for my husband to function as head of our family.

   ❑ I occasionally make it difficult for my husband to function as head of our family.

   ❑ I seldom make it difficult for my husband to function as head of our family.

   ❑ I never make it difficult for my husband to function as head of our family.

2. Wives, when was the last time you acknowledged your husband as leader of your home? When was the last time you thanked him for taking a leadership role and making important decisions for your family?

   _____

   _____

   _____

3. Husbands can't lead effectively unless their wives are good followers. Wives, write a prayer thanking God for the husband He has provided to lead your family and asking Him to enable you to be a good follower.

   _____

   _____

   _____

4. Do you pray daily for your spouse? Move your spouse to the top of your prayer list!

5. In Genesis 3:16, God prophesies women will desire to usurp man's authority over them, while men will seek to put women under their feet. Neither response is biblical nor in accordance with God's plan for man and woman. When you became a Christian, what were some of the tools with which God equipped you to live in harmony with your spouse?

Romans 5:5 _____

John 15:11 _____

Acts 5:32 _____

Philippians 4:5 _____

2 Timothy 1:7 _____

6. Each of us is accountable to God and responsible for our own thoughts, speech, and actions. Are there any ways in which you need to change your behavior to fulfill your marriage responsibilities of submission (wives) or leadership (husbands) the way God intended? Confess any sin to God and ask Him to give you a heart that willingly obeys His commands to you as a spouse and follower of Christ.

_____

_____

SUBMISSION: TO PLEASE THE LORD

Now, let's address the last phrase of Colossians 3:18: "…as is fitting in the Lord." One translation says, "…as is fitting for those who belong to the Lord" (NLT). Translated, the word *fitting* refers to a standard. In essence, Christian wives are to submit to their husbands because it is God's standard. The quickest way I know to misery and emptiness is to shortcut God's standard. Conversely, the quickest way to fulfillment is abiding by God's standard.

Paul wrote this letter to a society much like our own. Feminists were marching in Rome. Divorce was rampant. Paul wrote to the Christians, "Here is God's accepted standard. It works. Take your cues from God and do what is fitting in the Lord. Make God's standard your own."

Today's women, men, kids, and families are confronted with blurring roles in a unisex society. Without focused attention on God's Word and commitment to living His standard, women and men can easily become confused about their roles. Without strong modeling and teaching from parents, children can grow up unaware of who they are in God's eyes, who God has called them to be, and the roles He intends them to fill.

A wife writing to wives, author Barbara Rainey pens an analogy many wives will understand:

If you've ever sewn a dress or attempted to sew one, you know how a pattern works. The pattern is made of many pieces, some large, some small, none of which accurately resemble the finished product. When you lay out the pattern and cut the cloth, you don't have a garment, but only some scraps of cloth. But when it's properly fitted together, accord-

---

> ### 🏠 BUILDER'S NOTES
>
> *Without focused attention on God's Word and commitment to living His standard, women and men can easily become confused about their roles.*

ing to the pattern directions, and made useable with buttons, zippers, or snaps, these incomplete pieces make a whole dress. Every pattern has two pieces for every part, two sleeves, two bodice pieces, a front and back skirt, even a collar and facing pieces that are usually in twos. That's how it is in marriage. God has designed a master pattern for husbands and wives, that when followed will create a whole, useable, beautiful marriage. Just as the same dress pattern can be made into a wide variety of sizes and colors with numerous differences in detail, so my marriage may look different from yours. But both of us, if we acknowledge Christ as the Lord of our lives, must work out our marriages according to God's pattern. This key is for each wife to follow the divine pattern, to know her part, and how to fit it in with her husband's.[30]

Women and men, wives and husbands, take your cues from God's standard. Decide to do what "is fitting in the Lord."

Questions to Consider

1. For what primary reason should a wife submit to her husband?

   _____

2. A wife is to fill her role "as is fitting in the Lord" (Col. 3:18).

3. Based on Psalm 86:9, what is the purpose for which God created you?

   _____

   _____

4. According to the following Scriptures, there is a direct correlation between loving God and following His commandments. Complete each Scripture in the space provided.

   Exodus 20:5-6 "For I, the LORD your God... [show] mercy to thousands, to those who love Me and _____."

   John 14:15 "If you love Me, _____."

   John 15:10 "If you keep My commandments, you will _____."

5. How well do you keep God's commandments? Would it be obvious to anyone who examined your life that you love God? Identify one area of your life in which you may have stumbled or fallen spiritually. Write a prayer of confession and repentance. As you pray, remember God is "...faithful and just to forgive us our sins and to cleanse us from all unrighteousness"(1 John 1:9).

   _____

   _____

THE VIRTUOUS WIFE

Not only does Scripture provide us with Paul's instructions, but in Proverbs 31 we find a detailed example of the "virtuous wife." If any man has ever truly known women, it was the author of Proverbs, King Solomon. First Kings tells us he "…loved many foreign women…had seven hundred wives, princesses, and three hundred concubines; and his wives turned away his heart" (1 Kings 11:1, 3). Solomon was also a man of great wisdom; God told him, "…see, I have given you a wise and understanding heart, so that there has not been anyone like you before you, nor shall any like you arise after you" (1 Kings 3:12). Given his experience with women and the wisdom given to him by God, it's not surprising Solomon's writings include advice regarding women.

In the book of Proverbs, Solomon wrote, "An excellent wife is the crown of her husband, but she who causes shame is like rottenness in his bones" (Prov. 12:4). Twice he wrote, "It is better to dwell in a corner of a housetop, than in a house shared with a contentious woman" (Prov. 21:9, 25:24). Unquestionably, Solomon knew women well. However, though he authored Proverbs 31, its words were given to him by a woman: "The words of King Lemuel, the utterance which his mother taught him" (Prov. 31:1).

I believe Proverbs 31 is included in Scripture for two reasons: one, to provide young Jewish girls (and women today) with a role model of what a wife should be; and two, to teach young men what qualities to look for in a wife. Solomon wrote this passage not to condemn and incite guilt among women struggling to keep up with their responsibilities, but rather to extol the virtues of a godly wife and mother.

Beauty

Verses 10 through 31 of Proverbs 31 could easily be entitled "The Virtuous Wife" because they begin with the question, "Who can find a virtuous wife?" (Prov. 31:10), or "…a virtuous woman?" (KJV).

Put another way, the question might read: How do you measure the value of a woman? What characteristics make a woman valuable? If you posed this question to today's single men, the most common response would likely be along the lines of: "Looks, appearance. Personality, of course, but she's got to look good." Sadly, our world emphasizes the external when it comes to women. Look at the magazines by the checkout register in any store; that's the world's view of what a woman ought to be like.

Some time ago, I saw a television news program titled, "America's Obsession with Looks and Beauty." It was subtitled, "What People Cannot Live Without." The broadcast reported fashion mannequins are contributing to the mindset of what a woman should look like. According to sociologists and psychologists, the average mannequin is the size of an emaciated woman. Women and men see an outfit on a mannequin and say, "That looks great!" Yet, when most women try on the outfit, it doesn't look the same. Why? Because, thank God, most women are not emaciated!

God's description of a woman's worth and beauty is far different than the world's. Scripture tells us: "Do not let your adornment be merely outward—arranging the hair, wearing gold, or putting on fine apparel—rather let it be the hidden person of the heart, with the incorruptible beauty of a gentle and quiet spirit, which is very precious in the sight of God" (1 Pet. 3:3-4). God is not opposed to outward physical beauty; He invented it. However, what God emphasizes is very different than "merely outward" appearance.

Look at Proverbs 31:30: "Charm is deceitful and beauty is passing, but a woman who fears the LORD, she shall be praised." In the James Moffat Translation, the same verse reads: "Charms may wane and beauty wither, so keep your praise for a wife with brains."[31]

Do you see now why God doesn't emphasize outward physical beauty? It's called age. No matter how we try to preserve our bodies, they ultimately age. Thus, a woman whose beauty is merely outward is only temporarily beautiful. Conversely, a woman who possesses "the incorruptible beauty of a gentle and quiet spirit" and other characteristics of a godly woman, is a woman of lasting beauty—made gorgeous by her deeply developed character.

Questions to Consider

1. Proverbs 31:10 begins, "Who can find a virtuous wife?" Look up the word *virtue* in a dictionary and write the definition below:

   _____

   _____

2. According to 1 Peter 3:1-4, what are some characteristics and traits that comprise "the ideal woman" in God's sight? Read this Scripture and complete the blanks below.

   She is to be s_____ to her own husband.

   Her conduct is to be c_____.

   Her conduct is to be accompanied by f_____ (of the Lord).

   Her adornment is not to be merely outward, but is to be the h_____ p_____ of the h_____.

   She is to have a g_____ and q_____ spirit, which is very precious in the sight of God.

3. While man looks at outward appearances, God places more importance elsewhere. Read 1 Samuel 16:7. What does God look at? _____

4. Did you know when the word *beauty* is used in Scripture, it typically does not refer to man or woman? Read each Scripture below and identify the object described as possessing beauty.

1 Chronicles 16:29 _____

Psalm 50:2 _____

Psalm 90:17 _____

Psalm 96:6 _____

5. Women, on a scale of 0 to 10, with 0 being "not at all" and 10 being "at all times," rank yourselves on the following statements:

_____ I am a godly woman.

_____ I am a trustworthy woman.

_____ I am a devoted woman.

_____ I am a kindhearted woman.

These characteristics truly make a woman beautiful!

Godliness

If you're a single man wondering what to look for in a wife, look for a godly woman. Notice the end of Proverbs 31:30: "…a woman who fears the LORD, she shall be praised." Look for a woman whose first priority is her relationship with Jesus Christ. If you are a woman wondering, "What kind of a woman does God want me to be?", your answer is Proverbs 31:30: "…a woman who fears the LORD." Are you a busy wife and mother stretched in a million directions, wondering what to cut out of your life? Don't cut out your relationship with God; you will wither and wane without it.

Questions to Consider

1. The most important relationship a person needs to develop is his/her relationship with the Lord. According to the following Scriptures, what are some of the ways we can foster this most important relationship?

Psalm 1:2 _____

1 Corinthians 11:23-25 _____

1 Thessalonians 5:17 _____

Hebrews 6:10 _____

2. Verses 11-12 of Proverbs 31 talk about the virtuous woman's relationship with her husband. He "safely trusts her." She "does him good and not evil all the days of her life." Wives, do you seek specific ways to do good things

> **BUILDER'S NOTES**
>
> *"What kind of a woman does God want me to be?", your answer is Proverbs 31:30: "…a woman who fears the LORD."*

BUILDER'S NOTES

In this text, trustworthy literally means "someone who can be trusted to transact business correctly." A godly wife can be trusted to transact the business of her home.

for your husband? List two or three things you can do for your husband this week that will "do him good."

_____

_____

_____

Trustworthiness

The virtuous wife is trustworthy: "The heart of her husband safely trusts her…" (Prov. 31:11). Her husband has complete confidence in his wife. In this text, *trustworthy* literally means "someone who can be trusted to transact business correctly." A godly wife can be trusted to transact the business of her home. Her husband can trust her to be faithful to him morally, to spend her time wisely, and to make wise financial choices. As such, she becomes a constant source of encouragement and assurance to her husband and family.

Have you noticed all the traits described in Proverbs 31 are repeated in the New Testament as qualities of a godly wife? For example, "…wives are to be women worthy of respect, not malicious talkers but temperate and trustworthy in everything" (1 Tim. 3:11, NIV).

Questions to Consider

1. Wives, in what specific ways can your husband fully and completely trust you? Husbands, in what specific areas do you trust your wife? Check all that apply.

   ❑ Moral faithfulness

   ❑ Household finances

   ❑ Keeping appointments and commitments on time

   ❑ Completion of tasks in a timely manner

   ❑ Meeting the daily needs of my husband and children

   ❑ Other: _____

2. Proverbs 12:4 offers wives some wise counsel. Read this Scripture and write it below.

   _____

   _____

   _____

3. Wives, examine your hearts. Are there any areas in which you have failed to be completely trustworthy? Would your husband say, "I can trust my wife in

most areas, except…"? If appropriate, write a prayer to the Lord. Confess your sin(s) to Him. Ask Him to help you become a fully trustworthy wife to whom your husband can "entrust his own heart."

_____

_____

Devotion

Almost every verse of Proverbs 31:11-31 tells us the virtuous woman is devoted to her home and family. Let's compare this trait with Paul's New Testament writings regarding godly women: "[T]each the older women to be reverent in the way they live, not to be slanderers or addicted to much wine, but to teach what is good. Then they can train the younger women to love their husbands and children, to be self-controlled and pure, to be busy at home, to be kind, and to be subject to their husbands, so that no one will malign the Word of God" (Titus 2:3-5, NIV).

One of the characteristics Paul lists is "to be busy at home." For example, while raising young children, the virtuous woman described in Proverbs 31 shops, works with her hands, and provides food and clothing for her family and others (Prov. 31:13-15, 19-22, 27). Note that Paul does not say a woman cannot be active or have a career outside the home. The virtuous woman has a manufacturing business and real estate investment (Prov. 31:16, 24). Nor does Paul say women should do all the housework. The Proverbs 31 woman receives help from maidservants (Prov. 31:15).

Paul is addressing the issue of priorities. Though the godly woman may have activities outside the home, these must be subject to her primary priority: her home and family. When a woman becomes a wife, she accepts a God-ordained role in which home, husband, and family receive top billing.

I have a book in my study entitled *How to be a Happy Wife of an Unsaved Husband*. Its female author writes:

> At a recent parents' meeting, I raised my hand in response to a request for volunteers for a certain school project. My husband looked at me out of the corner of his eye and whispered, "Put that hand down right now!" I took this as divine guidance to pass on that project. In the past, I have resigned from good jobs for one or more of the above reasons and I've never regretted it. For what does it pay to gain the whole world and have your family life falling apart at the seams? God eventually provides all of my heart's desires if I am faithful to put family responsibilities ahead of my lust for new carpeting or the latest appliance.[32]

BUILDER'S NOTES

Though the godly woman may have activities outside the home, these must be subject to her primary priority: her home and family. When a woman becomes a wife, she accepts a God-ordained role in which home, husband and family receive top billing.

Questions to Consider

Paul gives advice for godly women in Titus 2:3-5. Answer the following questions related to this Scripture:

1. What does it mean to exhibit "reverent behavior"? _____

   _____

2. What is the definition of *slander?* _____

   _____

3. What seven things are young women admonished to do?

   a. _____

   b. _____

   c. _____

   d. _____

   e. _____

   f. _____

   g. _____

4. In Titus 2:5, what is the reason given for women to behave in this godly manner? _____

   _____

5. Women, how devoted are you to your family? Rank the following from 1 to 7, with 1 representing those to whom you are most devoted, and 7 indicating those to whom you are least devoted. Be honest as you examine your heart.

   _____ My Lord and Savior Jesus Christ

   _____ My husband

   _____ My children

   _____ My extended family (parents, siblings, etc.)

   _____ My friends

   _____ My fellow believers in ministry outside the home

   _____ My co-workers

6. Women, are needs at home going unmet while you are doing other things? Is your home disorganized? Is your family seeing enough of you? Take a moment to pray, asking God to help you answer these questions honestly. If

your priorities have become unbalanced, write one or two steps you can commit to take to bring home and family to their rightful place in your life.

_____

_____

_____

_____

Kindness

Another trait of the virtuous wife is kindheartedness. "She extends her hand to the poor, yes, she reaches out her hands to the needy" (Prov. 31:20). "She opens her mouth with wisdom, and on her tongue is the law of kindness" (Prov. 31:26).

Again, we see how beautifully Proverbs 31 and the New Testament complement each other. Returning to our earlier Titus reference, we see it says, "…train the younger women…to be kind…so that no one will malign the Word of God" (Titus 2:4-5, NIV).

I have found that kindhearted women always have a ministry. In addition, they are loved by many. Others flock to women who are kindhearted and make time to encourage, help, or share with others.

The book of Acts tells us of a woman called Dorcas who loved the poor and gave to others of what she had. When she died, women came to her funeral holding robes and beautiful clothing Dorcas had made for them with love.[33] What a testimony of a virtuous woman: one who was generous and kindhearted, trustworthy and devoted to her family.

Questions to Consider

Proverbs 31:20 says of the virtuous woman, "She extends her hand to the poor, yes, she reaches out her hands to the needy." Based on the Scripture references given, answer the following questions regarding kindness.

1. According to Luke 6:35, how are we to be kind as the Most High is kind?

_____

2. How does 1 Corinthians 13:4 define *love?* _____

_____

3. According to Ephesians 4:32, how are we to treat one another? _____

4. Matthew 25:35-36 lists several things a kindhearted person might do for one in need. In verse 40 of the same chapter, Jesus says that if you have been kindhearted to one of the least of His brethren, to whom have you truly ministered? _____

5. Proverbs 31:26 says of the virtuous woman, "She opens her mouth with wisdom, and on her tongue is the law of kindness." Sometimes we open our mouths and out comes…not wisdom. What do the following Scriptures say about our words and our speech?

Proverbs 10:19 _____

Proverbs 12:25 _____

Proverbs 16:24 _____

Proverbs 27:2 _____

THE VIRTUOUS WIFE'S REWARD

You may be asking, "What does a woman get after putting in that kind of a lifetime?" Her reward is twofold: she influences lives, and she receives praise.

Godly Influence

A virtuous woman is a godly influence for her husband and children. "Her husband is known in the gates, when he sits among the elders of the land" (Prov. 31:23). Let me describe what that means.

The business place of every old city was at its gates—the entrance to the city. Men gathered here to conduct business, settle legal matters, and talk. This woman's character influenced her husband in such a way that he was enabled to occupy a prominent position. His position was part of her reward. In addition, some of the conversation at the gates was about her: "Give her of the fruit of her hands, and let her own works praise her in the gates" (Prov. 31:31). Her works were spoken about in the city's place of importance; she was quite an influence for her husband.

Let's skip back to the beginning. After God created the world, He made man. And after He made man, He said, "It is not good that man should be alone; I will make him a helper comparable to him" (Gen. 2:18). In the Hebrew language, *a helper comparable to him* essentially meant "someone who will bring complete fullness, a companion, and influence." God recognized that alone, man is not complete; he needs a woman to complete him. From the beginning, God intended marriage to bring fullness and completeness, not reduction or restriction.

I can't tell you how much my wife, Lenya, has influenced my life. Some of my greatest sermon ideas have come from her. She has influenced the way I think, even about the Lord. If I am in any way successful or make an impact today, a lot of it is due to her influence on my life.

Praise

In addition to influence, the virtuous woman receives a second reward: affirmation, attention, and affection from her family. "Her children rise up and call her blessed; her husband also, and he praises her: 'Many daughters have done well, but you excel them all'" (Prov. 31:28-29).

Kids don't always "call [their mother] blessed" when they're young. Instead, when Mom spanks them, they say, "I don't like you!" Or they rebel during the teenage years. Hang in there, Mom. If you're doing your job right, the blessing will come. If a mother possesses and faithfully cultivates the characteristics of a virtuous woman, her children will bless her when they begin to understand all she invested in them.

BUILDER'S NOTES

Husbands, rise up and call your wives blessed. Your children may be too young, but you are fully able to understand how much your wife invests in you.

As an adult, do you call your own mother blessed? Or are you estranged from your mom and dad for some reason? Call them today and tell them, "Regardless of what's gone on in the past, I'm determined to love, respect, and honor you. I call you blessed."

Husbands, rise up and call your wives blessed. Your children may be too young, but you are fully able to understand how much your wife invests in you. God created her to complete you and gave her to you as your wife. Tell and show her you love her until she says, "I heard that already forty times today."

Proverbs 31 and Ephesians 5 tell us a wife's reward is also her husband's reward in many ways, and vice versa.[34] Here are some other statistics that might interest you: Husbands who kiss their wives every morning before leaving for work usually live five years longer than those who do not. A kissing husband has fewer automobile accidents, loses up to 50 percent less time from work because of illness, and earns 30 percent to 40 percent more than a nonkissing husband. Tune up that pucker, guys!

Questions to Consider

1. Wives, has your influence over your husband elevated him or crippled him? Is he respected and admired in part by the role you play in his life? Determine today that your character will elevate your husband in the eyes of his children, parents, friends, co-workers, and boss.

2. The Lord promises rewards to His children who obey Him. In the following Scriptures, what rewards are promised to those who walk in His ways?

The crown of _____
(2 Tim. 4:8)

The crown of _____
(Jas. 1:12)

The crown of _____
(1 Pet. 5:4)

3. In addition to rewards from the Lord, the virtuous woman can also expect rewards from her husband and her children.

According to Proverbs 31:28, her children do what? _____

_____

According to Proverbs 31:29, what does her husband say about her? _____

_____

4. The woman in Proverbs 31 had a husband and children who appreciated her—and let her know it. How well have you been expressing your appreciation for your wife and/or mother? Write a prayer to God today, asking Him to give you an opportunity this week to express your appreciation to a godly wife or mother.

_____

_____

_____

GOD'S REWARD

*W*ebster's *Dictionary* defines a child this way: "an unborn or recently born person; a young person especially between infancy and youth; a son or daughter of human parents." To me, these definitions fall far short of describing the miracle a child is and the value he or she represents. In fact, I believe few people think of children solely in terms of age or biology. Positively or negatively, directly and indirectly, people view children in many different ways: blessings, burdens, responsibilities, miracles, accidents, challenges, dependents, possessions, adventures, teachers. God, too, uses several terms to describe children: heritage, inheritance, gift, assignment, reward, arrows. Through His Word, God makes it clear He desires us to see children through His eyes and that He holds us responsible for treating them with special care.

A Heritage

Psalm 127 tells us, "Behold, children are a heritage from the LORD, the fruit of the womb is a reward. Like arrows in the hand of a warrior, so are the children of one's youth. Happy is the man who has his quiver full of them…"
(Ps. 127:3-5a). The term *heritage* used in this verse means "possession, property, portion, inheritance."[35] Several translations use the term "gift" (NAS, NLT, NCV). One translation uses the term "assignment." I like that. Just when you thought school was over, God says, "Here's an assignment for you. Here's a child to be molded like clay. This child is your heritage, your assignment from Me."

From this verse, we learn that children initially belong to God. They are His to create and His to give. He gives them to us, along with the responsibility to care for them as He did before giving them to us.

A Reward

Psalm 127:3 also says children are a reward. Make a note of that. They're not an accident, curse, or inconvenience. They're a reward. What a difference I believe we would see in our children if all parents treated them as a reward.

Let me note for those who know couples who are unable to, or who have chosen not to, have children, children are not God's only reward. God rewards His sons and daughters in many different, creative ways designed specifically for the individual plans He has for each of us.

Arrows

Psalm 127:4 says, "Like arrows in the hand of a warrior, so are the children of one's youth." God calls children "arrows." What do you do with an arrow? You shoot it at a target. This verse tells us children are to be launched like an arrow with a target in mind. The target: God and His specific will for their lives.

Sadly, many parents fail to see the target. We fail to study our children to see what gifts and calling God has put within them. We fail to encourage them to develop their God-given talents. God calls us to prepare, draw, and launch our "arrows" as He directs us in His Word.

BUILDER'S NOTES

Every child is uniquely created and intimately known by God. "Fearfully and wonderfully made," each child has a unique temperament, a unique personality, a unique set of abilities, and a unique plan designed by God.

Valued by God

We also know children are important and valuable to Jesus, who gave several specific commands regarding children, including: "Let the little children come to Me, and do not forbid them; for of such is the kingdom of heaven" (Matt. 19:14). He also said, "...It is not the will of your Father who is in heaven that one of these little ones should perish" (Matt. 18:14).

Four hundred years before Jesus Christ, the philosopher Socrates commented on the Greeks' propensity to throw away children, then regarded as dispensable and secondary to professions and wealth. Socrates said, "Could I climb the highest place in Athens, I would lift up my voice and proclaim, 'Fellow citizens, why do you turn and scrape every stone to gather wealth and take so little care of your children to whom you must one day relinquish all?'" What a powerful indictment of ancient Greece and modern America.

Uniquely Created by God

Every child is uniquely created and intimately known by God. "Fearfully and wonderfully made," each child has a unique temperament, a unique personality, a unique set of abilities, and a unique plan designed by God. Psalm 139 tells us:

For You formed my inward parts; You covered me in my mother's womb. I will praise You, for I am fearfully and wonderfully made; Marvelous are Your works, and that my soul knows very well. My frame was not hidden from You, when I was made in secret, and skillfully wrought in the lowest parts of the earth. Your eyes saw my substance, being yet unformed. And in Your book they all were written, the days fashioned for me, when as yet there were none of them. Ps. 139:13-16

Human

As different as they are from each other, all children have one thing in common: a self-assertive nature that must be broken.

Jeremiah tells us, "The heart is deceitful above all things, and desperately wicked…" (Jer. 17:9). Paul writes in Romans, "As the Scriptures say, 'No one is good—not even one.'" (Rom. 3:10, NLT); and later, "…Through one man sin entered the world, and death through sin, and thus death spread to all men, because all sinned" (Rom. 5:12). David writes, "For I was born a sinner—yes, from the moment my mother conceived me" (Ps. 51:5, NLT). The moment each of us was conceived by our parents, we inherited a sinful nature.

As I've watched my son grow, I've thought, "God, it's wonderful to see the development processes You've created within my son. He is indeed 'fearfully and wonderfully made.'" Yet, deep within my son's heart, there's a sinful nature that is corrupt to the core.

As you read this, you might be thinking, "Not my kid." Let me ask this: Did you ever have to teach your child to disobey? Did you ever have to say: "Now, son, you're a little too good. In fact, you're almost perfect. Give the other kids a break. Here, let me tell you how to sin a little bit. I'm good at it"? On the contrary, kids need to be taught to obey, love, and share unselfishly because the other things come so naturally.

In Need of God

Because each of us is born with a depraved nature that needs redemption, the Bible speaks about our need for new birth. Jesus said, "That which is born of the flesh is flesh, and that which is born of the Spirit is spirit" (John 3:6).

Questions to Consider

1. What does Jesus tell us in the following Scriptures about how He wants us to treat children?

   Matt. 10:42 _____

   Matt. 18:10 _____

   Mark 9:42 _____

BUILDER'S NOTES

2. Each of us is born with a sin nature, which includes a bent toward disobedience. Look up each of the following Scriptures and complete the thoughts below.

Although God created me in His own image (Gen. 1:27), I can _____

_____ (John 15:5).

Although I am fearfully and wonderfully made (Ps. 139:14), my heart

_____ (Jer. 17:9).

Although God made me a little lower than the angels (Ps. 8:5), _____

my flesh _____ (Gal. 5:17).

Because of Jesus' atoning death on the cross, I can "reckon [myself] to be

_____" (Rom. 6:11).

3. Note what the following Scriptures say about:

A New Birth

John 1:12-13 _____

Romans 6:8 _____

1 Peter 1:23 _____

1 John 5:4 _____

A New Nature

2 Corinthians 5:17 _____

Ephesians 4:24 _____

Colossians 3:9-10 _____

2 Peter 1:4 _____

A New Heart

Ezekiel 36:26-27 _____

Psalm 24:4-5 _____

Matthew 5:8 _____

Hebrews 10:22 _____

OBEDIENCE: A CHILD'S ROLE

God's primary instructions to children, we find, are regarding their relationship with their parents. The fifth of the Ten Commandments is, "Honor your father and your mother, that your days may be long upon the land which the LORD your God is giving you" (Ex. 20:12). Scripture repeats this commandment no less than eight times.[36] In his letter to the Colossians, Paul wrote, "Children, obey your parents in all things, for this is well pleasing to the Lord" (Col. 3:20). To the Ephesians, he instructed, "Children, obey your parents in the Lord, for this is right." (Eph. 6:1).

The word *children* in the latter two verses is translated from the Greek word *teknon*, which refers to all offspring of any age. Since every person is the child of two parents, and every Christian is a child of God (John 1:12), Paul's message in Colossians 3:20 is to all of us.

As parents, our responsibility to heed Paul's instructions to children is great. Our children see us as role models of how they ought to be. If I treat my parents with disrespect, my children will observe this and model their behavior toward me from the way they see me treating my parents. In addition, because we teach our children that God is our heavenly Father, children also model their behavior toward us as parents from the way they see us responding to God. When our children see us thanking God, looking to God's Word for instruction, and living our lives the way God's Word tells us to, they see an example of how they ought to respond to us as parents.

What Obedience Is

Notice the word *obey* is four letters long. To both kids and adults, *obey* is often considered a "four-letter word," in that phrase's most negative sense. Why? As a result of the sinful nature with which we are born, our bodies are naturally wired for defiance and independence—not obedience. Nonetheless, obedience is God's key instruction to children.

The word for *obey* used in Colossians 3:20 is translated from the Greek term *hupakouo*, which means "to hear or to listen." It's the word God used when He said to Abraham: "In your seed all the nations of the earth shall be blessed, because you have obeyed My voice" (Gen. 22:18). Obedience first requires listening to the one giving instruction and then doing what is instructed.

We also learn obedience is "well pleasing to the Lord." There's a certain stage in a child's life when Mom and Dad are perfect. Then the child grows up and enters the stage in which he or she believes Mom and Dad are the dumbest people on earth. Parents, it's not fun for either you or your kids to enforce your children's obedience during this stage—especially when families around you are adopting more lenient standards. Nonetheless, God's Word gives you at least two reasons to persevere in maintaining a standard of obedience from your kids: "…for this is well pleasing to the Lord" (Col. 3:20), and "Train up a child in the way he should go, and when he is old he will not depart from it" (Prov. 22:6). The Bible also gives children a reason for obeying and honoring their parents: "Honor your father and your mother, as the LORD your God has

BLUEPRINTS

The word for obey used in Colossians 3:20 is translated from the Greek term hupakouo, which means "to hear or to listen."

commanded you, that your days may be long, and that it may be well with you…" (Deut. 5:16).

Not only is obedience well pleasing to God, but we also know it is important to Him. Parental respect is so important to God that several Old Testament writings are devoted to it. In the book of Proverbs, Solomon writes: "My son, hear the instruction of your father, and do not forsake the law of your mother" (Prov. 1:8). A few chapters later, we read, "My son, keep my words, and treasure my commands within you. Keep my commands and live, and my law as the apple of your eye" (Prov. 7:1-2). Do you know what the apple of your eye is? It's your eyeball—an area of the body so sensitive that contact with a small speck of dust can painfully render a person virtually helpless. For most of us, almost everything we do each day is to some degree dependent on proper function of our eyes. Our society calls people permanently without the use of their eyes "visually handicapped" or "visually disabled." In Proverbs 7:2, Solomon tells us to guard, treasure, and protect godly teaching given to us by our parents—authorities God has placed in our lives—as carefully as we protect our eyes from harm.

Why is obedience to one's parents so important? Solomon tells us: "My son, keep your father's command, and do not forsake the law of your mother. Bind them continually upon your heart; tie them around your neck. When you roam, they will lead you; when you sleep, they will keep you; and when you awake, they will speak with you. For the commandment is a lamp, and the law a light; reproofs of instruction are the way of life" (Prov. 6:20-23). God's instruction to children through their parents provides both direction and protection for the rest of their lives.

BUILDER'S NOTES

Why is obedience to one's parents so important? God's instruction to children through their parents provides both direction and protection for the rest of their lives.

Questions to Consider

1. Since every Christian is a child of God, Paul's instructions in Colossians 3:20 apply to our relationship with God as well as His with our earthly parents. What do the following Scriptures say about obedience?

   Deuteronomy 12:28 _____

   Jeremiah 38:20 _____

   Acts 5:29 _____

   2 Corinthians 10:5 _____

   Hebrews 5:8 _____

2. According to Colossians 3:20, why are children to obey their parents?

   _____

   _____

3. To many, the word *obey* is a negative word. Using the Scriptures listed below, fill in the blanks to create an acronym for *obey*.

O _____

(Leviticus 19:37)

B _____

(1 John 3:23)

E _____

(1 Thessalonians 3:13)

Y _____

(2 Chronicles 30:8)

4. What does Proverbs 3:11-12 say to all of God's children?

_____

5. Read Exodus 20:12. The fifth of the Ten Commandments carries a promise to those who honor their father and their mother. What is that promise?

_____

_____

_____

6. Read Psalm 119:105.

How are God's commandments like a lamp? _____

How are His laws like a light? _____

WHAT OBEDIENCE ISN'T

Perfection: Obedience is not synonymous with perfect performance. Note something, parents: The one instruction given to children in Colossians 3:20 is to obey their parents. God does not command children to succeed or be perfect. Whatever you instruct your children to do, if they listen to you and try to follow your instructions, they have done the one thing for which God holds them responsible. Children are not obligated to fulfill your expectations of them; they are simply responsible for doing, to the best of their ability, what you ask them to do.

Overriding God's Authority: Secondly, obedience to one's parents does not take priority over obeying God. Notice the phrases "well pleasing to the Lord" (Col. 3:20) and "in the Lord" (Eph. 6:1). These words remind us that pleasing God is every person's highest responsibility. Elsewhere in the New Testament Jesus said, "He who loves father or mother more than Me is not worthy of Me"

(Matt. 10:37). Jesus was not saying, "I want to break up your home." He wants your home to be one of unity and reconciliation. Instead, Jesus was telling us strife is inevitable when one family member knows the Lord and another doesn't.

Many of us have encountered situations in which our parents' instruction conflicted with God's commands. Or perhaps we have disagreed with our children when they have told us they believe they are led by God to do a certain thing. What should we do when this happens? We find some examples in Acts.

"So [the Sanhedrin] called [Peter and John] and commanded them not to speak at all nor teach in the name of Jesus. But Peter and John answered and said to them, 'Whether it is right in the sight of God to listen to you more than to God, you judge. For we cannot but speak the things which we have seen and heard'" (Acts 4:18-20). The story continues in Acts chapter 5: "When [the Sanhedrin] had brought [the apostles], they set them before the council. And the high priest asked them, saying, 'Did we not strictly command you not to teach in this name? And look, you have filled Jerusalem with your doctrine, and intend to bring this Man's blood on us!' But Peter and the other apostles answered and said: 'We ought to obey God rather than men'" (Acts 5:27-29).

The word *ought* is a translation of a Greek word which means "necessary" or "must." When a person is given a command that violates his or her conscience before God, he or she must obey God. God's Word tells children to obey their parents "in all things" (Col. 3:20), but He also tells them to obey their parents "in the Lord, for this is right" (Eph. 6:1).

When I became a Christian, the first people I wanted to tell were my parents. I love my parents deeply and had a good relationship with them as I grew up. I figured they would be as elated as I was about my Christianity. Instead, they were insulted and angry. They told me not to go to church or Bible studies, read my Bible or pray. However, when a parent overrides God's instruction in His Word, he or she usurps God's prerogative. Because my parents' instruction to me contradicted God's, my response to them had to be something like this: "I love you, respect you, and will continue to obey you. I'll do my chores and whatever you ask me to at home. But I can't let you intrude on my relationship with the Lord. If I need to leave your house, I will, but I have to obey God rather than man."

Before we were married, my wife Lenya worked for Youth With a Mission. Her father wasn't excited about her leaving home, but he agreed. After serving for a while, she came home and asked her father for permission to return as a member of the YWAM staff. Though a Christian, he denied her request. Frustrated, Lenya called the base director and told him, "My dad says I can't serve the Lord on the mission field, but I feel like God told me to do it." Her director said, "Stay home." She protested. "What do you mean stay home? I'll

---

BUILDER'S NOTES

When a person is given a command that violates his or her conscience before God, he or she must obey God. God's Word tells children to obey their parents "in all things" (Col. 3:20), but He also tells them to obey their parents "in the Lord, for this is right" (Eph. 6:1).

be disobeying God." He responded, "No, your dad may be disobeying God. Submit to him and lay the burden of responsibility for that choice on his shoulders." She didn't like it, but she did it. A miserable day or so later, her dad came to her and said, "I don't want to be the one responsible for you disobeying God. You can go." God's Word was followed, and God's will was done.

Finding Loopholes

Where would you first look in Scripture for strong examples of strict obedience to God and adherence to His commands? If I didn't know better, I'd probably turn to God's chosen people, the Jews. After all, they're the ones to whom God personally gave His laws. And they were the ones keeping tabs on Jesus during the time He spent on earth.

In some respects, I'd be right on the money if I looked to the Jews for examples of children's obedience to parents. Jewish culture expected children to respect and obey their parents. Paul capitalized on this when he wrote the same instructions to the Ephesians. However, the Pharisees had corrupted God's laws regarding parental obedience into something God had not intended. Here's how the Pharisees' loophole system worked: Let's say a mother and father didn't have a couch and couldn't afford to buy one. They visited their son's or daughter's house and noticed their child had three couches. So the parents asked their child if they could borrow or have one of the couches. According to Pharisee law, the child could say, "Oh, that's Corban." In other words, "That's dedicated to God. I can't let you have it." Selfishly, yet under the guise of spirituality, Jewish men and women dedicated all kinds of things to the Lord so they had nothing to give to their parents.

Rebuking the Pharisees for twisting God's laws, Jesus told them, "...well did Isaiah prophesy of you hypocrites, as it is written: 'This people honors Me with their lips, but their heart is far from Me. And in vain they worship Me, teaching as doctrines the commandments of men.' For laying aside the commandment of God, you hold the tradition of men...All too well you reject the commandment of God, that you may keep your tradition. For Moses said, 'Honor your father and your mother'; and, 'He who curses father or mother, let him be put to death.' But you say, 'If a man says to his father or mother, "Whatever profit you might have received from me is Corban" ' (that is, a gift to God), then you no longer let him do anything for his father or his mother, making the Word of God of no effect through your tradition which you have handed down..." (Mark 7:6-13).

Even among those who openly claimed to be the most spiritually devout, we find disobedience and disrespect for parents. That's why Jesus said, "Unless your righteousness exceeds the righteousness of the scribes and Pharisees, you will by no means enter the kingdom of heaven" (Matt. 5:20).

BUILDER'S NOTES

Even among those who openly claimed to be the most spiritually devout, we find disobedience and disrespect for parents. That's why Jesus said, "[U]nless your righteousness exceeds the righteousness of the scribes and Pharisees, you will by no means enter the kingdom of heaven" (Matt. 5:20).

Questions to Consider

1. While kids should be given appropriate responsibilities at appropriate stages of their growth, they should not be expected to behave and react like grownups. What do you expect from your children? Consider the following:

	Always	Sometimes	Never
I allow my child time to just play.	❑	❑	❑
I expect my child to sit still and be quiet.	❑	❑	❑
I give my child lengthy, complicated instructions.	❑	❑	❑
I speak to my child in words he/she can understand.	❑	❑	❑
I allow my child to be silly and giggly.	❑	❑	❑
I let my child express his/her feelings without belittling them.	❑	❑	❑

2. Parents, are you guilty of trying to force your child into a mold, one *you* have decided is perfect for them? Do you accept and appreciate the character traits that make your child unique? If not, pen a prayer to the Lord, asking for His forgiveness. Commit to loving your child in a manner pleasing to *your* Father.

_____

_____

_____

3. When another person gives us a command that violates our conscience before God, who are we to obey? _____

4. Jesus anticipated that belief in Him would bring strife into our lives. Look up the following Scriptures and fill in the blanks below.

Matthew 10:34-37 "Do not think that I came to bring peace on earth. I did not come to bring peace but a _____. For I have come to 'set a man against his _____, a daughter against her _____, and a daughter-in-law against her _____'; and 'a man's enemies will be those _____.' He who loves _____or _____ more than Me is not worthy of Me. And he who loves _____ or _____ more than Me is not worthy of Me."

Mark 13:11-13 "But when they arrest you and deliver you up, do not worry beforehand, or premeditate what you will speak. But whatever is given you in that hour, speak that; for it is not you who speak, but the _____. Now brother will betray_____to death, and a father his _____; and children will rise up against_____ and cause them to be put to death. And you will be hated by all for My name's sake. But he who endures to the end _____."

John 16:33 "These things I have spoken to you, that in Me you may have peace. In the world you will have _____; but be of good cheer, I have overcome the world."

5. Matthew 10:36 says, "...a man's enemies will be those of his own household." In Matthew 5:44, how did Christ command us to treat our enemies?

_____

_____

6. A child must balance obedience to the Lord with obedience to parents. Read the following Scriptures and write them below.
Matthew 10:37 _____

_____

Acts 5:29 _____

_____

7. What do each of the following Proverbs tell children about instruction received from parents?
Proverbs 1:8 _____

_____

Proverbs 5:1 _____

_____

Proverbs 6:20 _____

_____

Proverbs 23:26 _____

_____

8. Many of God's commandments have been drastically distorted by the world's philosophies. Based on the Scripture references below, complete the following statements:

Matthew 19:9—Regarding adultery, God's Word says: _____

_____

Romans 1:26-27—Regarding homosexuality, God's Word says: _____

_____

Colossians 3:20 – Regarding "child rights," God's Word says: _____

Ephesians 5:3 – Regarding sex outside of marriage, God's Word says: _____

Psalm 139:13-16 – Regarding the unborn, God's Word says: _____

9. Read and study Mark 7:5-13. What do you suppose was the original intent of the practice of declaring certain things "Corban" or "dedicated"? _____

DISOBEDIENCE AND REBELLION

Today's society bears little respect for authority. As author Anatole Broyard said, "There was a time when we expected nothing of our children but obedience, as opposed to the present, when we expect everything of them but obedience." The status quo has changed from parents making the rules, setting schedules, and running the home, to children telling their parents what to do. Yet, God's Word tells us the dynamic in the home should be the other way around: "Train up a child in the way he should go…" (Prov. 22:6). If children didn't need training, God's Word wouldn't include this verse. Parents should be setting direction and calling the shots, not their children. Our society needs an authority overhaul—starting with the home.

God's View

God doesn't view disobedience lightly. In the book of Exodus, He told Israel not once, but twice: "[H]e who strikes (or curses) his father or his mother shall surely be put to death" (Ex. 21:15, 17). In the book of Leviticus, God again told Moses, "Everyone who curses his father or his mother shall surely be put to death. He has cursed his father or his mother. His blood shall be upon him" (Lev. 20:9).

In the book of Deuteronomy, we find further instruction from God regarding rebellious children: "If a man has a stubborn and rebellious son who will not obey the voice of his father or the voice of his mother, and who, when they have chastened him, will not heed them, then his father and his mother shall take hold of him and bring him out to the elders of his city, to the gate of his city. And they shall say to the elders of his city, 'This son of ours is stubborn and rebellious; he will not obey our voice; he is a glutton and a drunkard.' Then all the men of his city shall stone him to death with stones; so you shall put away the evil from among you, and all Israel shall hear and fear" (Deut. 21:18-21).

Proverbs provides yet another strong illustration: "There is a generation that curses its father, and does not bless its mother…The eye that mocks his father, and scorns obedience to his mother, the ravens of the valley will pick it out, and the young eagles will eat it" (Prov. 30:11, 17).

In Romans chapter 1, we find "disobedient to parents" in Paul's list of "those things which are not fitting" (Rom. 1:28). The list includes: "being filled with all unrighteousness, sexual immorality, wickedness, covetousness, maliciousness; full of envy, murder, strife, deceit, evil-mindedness; they are whisperers, back-biters, haters of God, violent, proud, boasters, inventors of evil things, disobedient to parents, undiscerning, untrustworthy, unloving, unforgiving, unmerciful" (Rom. 1:29-31). In fact, verse 32 tells us these things are not only "not fitting" in God's sight, but "…knowing the righteous judgment of God that those who practice such things are deserving of death." "Sexual immorality… murder…disobedient to parents." In God's eyes, disobedience to one's parents is as offensive as murder.

The home is God's training ground for teaching His children—parents and children alike—to serve Him as Christian soldiers and Christ followers. Home is where children learn to live the basic precepts of Christianity, including obedience. Many adults struggle with submitting to the Lord because they never learned to obey their parents. Yet, how can God grow us if we can't or won't obey Him? Obedience and growth are inseparably linked.

Parents' View
Parents do not respond well to children's defiance. Solomon writes in the book of Proverbs: "[A] wise son makes a glad father, but a foolish son is the grief of his mother" (Prov. 10:1). When children disregard their parents' authority, they break their parents' hearts.

Questions to Consider
1. Often we tend to think of sins in degrees, categorizing murder and adultery as "big" sins, and envy, gossip, etc. as "smaller" sins. This way of thinking opposes the Bible's teaching in James 2:10. What does James tell us about sin in any form?

   _____

   _____

   _____

BUILDER'S NOTES

The home is God's training ground for teaching His children— parents and children alike—to serve Him as Christian soldiers and Christ followers. Home is where children learn to live the basic precepts of Christianity, including obedience. Obedience and growth are inseparably linked.

2. Look up the word *respect* in a dictionary and write its definition. _____

    _____

    _____

3. What does God's Word say about *respect* and being "respectful"?

    Psalm 40:4 _____

    Isaiah 17:7 _____

    Ephesians 5:33 _____

    Hebrews 12:9 _____

4. Based on the following Scriptures, how does God feel about rebellion in the hearts of His children? See 2 Samuel 23:6, Proverbs 17:11, and Jeremiah 28:16. _____

    _____

    _____

    _____

Fathers

GOD'S CHOSEN GUIDES

ROLE CALL

In his book entitled *The Third Wave,* Alvin Toffler wrote, "Our civilization is experiencing a crisis, for there is a blurring of the traditional expectations between a man and a woman."

One factor blurring those expectations is a pervasive trend toward passivity among husbands and fathers. Some men fill leadership roles at work, but fail to budget enough time and energy to fill their God-given roles as leaders at home. Our society expects men to be absent from the home from early morning until late evening or night five or six days a week. Those long hours drain his energy and creativity, leaving him with nothing to give when he reaches home. Still other fathers have tried to lead their families, but eventually yielded to strong wives who have taken the reins and will not let go.

These patterns render lasting, life-shaping results. Whenever parental roles are blurred, confusion results, leaving children with no healthy role models. To prevent this from happening, we as parents—especially husbands and fathers—must look to God's Word for foundational principles and instruction. To develop and enjoy fulfilling relationships and happy families, we must build our lives upon these essential truths. They provide the blueprint for the husband and father God wants each man to be.

A Man and His God

Scripture tells us a man is to be the leader of his home and God is to be Lord of a man's life. To effectively lead, a man must know God and depend on Him daily for wisdom and instruction. Through relationship with God the Father, a man learns how to raise his children. Through relationship with Jesus Christ,

Bridegroom of the Church, a man learns how to love and lead his wife as a godly husband.

Abraham and His God

God's relationship with Abraham exemplifies the relationship God desires to have with every man. Speaking of Abraham, God said, "For I have known him, in order that he may command his children and his household after him, that they keep the way of the LORD, to do righteousness and justice, that the LORD may bring to Abraham what He has spoken to him." (Gen. 18:19).

The meaning of the phrase "I have known him" is "to have known by observation and experience." Other versions say, "I have chosen him" (NIV, NASB, NCV), "I have singled him out" (NLT), and "I have made him Mine." In essence, God is saying, "I have a relationship with Abraham for a purpose." Publicly, Abraham's life would influence nations of the world. Privately, Abraham would pass on a spiritual heritage to his children. One of God's primary purposes for relationship with Abraham was to equip him to command his children and household effectively.

BUILDER'S NOTES

A man who enjoys a strong, loving relationship with his heavenly Father provides a wonderful example for his wife and his children.

Real Men Love Jesus

A man who enjoys a strong, loving relationship with his heavenly Father provides a wonderful example for his wife and his children. Unfortunately, families in which Dad is really the spiritual leader are surprisingly rare. In too many homes, Mom is the spiritual leader while Dad limits his leadership to other areas. Counselor Paul Anderson once said, "As the substitute father for hundreds of youths over the past thirteen years, I have yet to encounter a young person in trouble whose difficulty could not be traced to the lack of a strong father image in the home."

Dr. James Dobson has written several books on spiritual leadership of the family. Dr. Dobson stresses a man's responsibility to assume spiritual leadership so he can shape a spiritual heritage for his family. He writes:

> It is my guess that 90 percent of the divorces that occur each year
> involve at least some of the elements described: an extremely busy hus-
> band who is in love with his work and who tends to be somewhat insen-
> sitive, unromantic, and non-communicative, married to a lonely, vulner-
> able, romantic woman who has severe doubts about her worth as a
> human being. They become a matched team: he works like a horse and
> she nags.[37]

Dr. Dobson also describes a letter he received after speaking at a conference:

> Will you please discuss this? Dad arrives home, reads the newspaper,
> eats dinner, talks on the phone, watches T.V., takes a shower, and goes to
> bed. This is a constant daily routine. It never changes. On Sunday, we

do go to church and then come home. We take a nap, then it's back to work on Monday morning. Our daughter is nine, we are not communicating, and our life is speeding by in this monotonous routine.[38]

What happens when the leader of a home fails to lead spiritually? The family declines. What happens when the family declines? The entire nation declines. President Dwight D. Eisenhower once said, "The problems of America are just family problems multiplied a million-fold."

Why does so much depend on Dad? Why are we placing spiritual leadership squarely on his shoulders?

A child's view of God depends largely on his father. We teach our children to call God "Father." A child's relationship with his father directly colors his view of God, either negatively or positively.

Some dads have daughters who will grow up, date, and marry. Young girls look to their father as an example of the kind of man they ought to marry.

Some dads have sons who will grow up, date, and marry. Boys need a role model of the kind of husband and father they should strive to become.

Recently a study was conducted among a number of families identified as having successful, happy homes. Six hundred participants were asked to list the main ingredients of a successful marriage and family. The number one answer was a Christ-centered home. Next was demonstration of committed love between mother and father. Third was demonstration of committed love between parents and children.

The most important thing a man can do for his family is love God with all his heart, mind, soul, and strength. I challenge you to consider whether or not Jesus Christ is the center of your life.

Questions to Consider

1. In a few words, describe your relationship with God. Is it solid? Is it personal? What place does your relationship with God hold in your day, your week, your life? Do you need to make any changes; if so, which ones?

_____

_____

_____

_____

_____

_____

_____

BUILDER'S NOTES

A child's view of God depends largely on his father. We teach our children to call God "Father." A child's relationship with his father directly colors his view of God, either negatively or positively.

2. Husbands, what kind of leader are you in your home? Would you describe yourself as passive and complacent, strong and effective, or somewhere in between? What steps do you need to take to ensure the growth and strength of your leadership at home? _____

_____

_____

_____

3. Wives, are you a helper or a hindrance to your husband in his role as leader of your home? In what ways can you support him as he leads you and your children?

_____

_____

_____

4. God singled out Abraham with two purposes in mind: to influence nations and to pass on a spiritual heritage to his children. What purposes might God have for your life?

_____

_____

_____

5. Besides a Christ-centered home, list three ingredients of a successful marriage and family.

_____

_____

_____

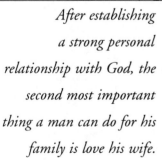

BUILDER'S NOTES

After establishing a strong personal relationship with God, the second most important thing a man can do for his family is love his wife.

A Man and His Wife

After establishing a strong personal relationship with God, the second most important thing a man can do for his family is love his wife. Several years ago, Dr. Clayton Bell said something that caught my attention. He said, "My father gave his children the best gift a father can give to his kids. He loved their mother."

The Real You

Ephesians chapter 5 tells us the same thing we learned in Genesis 18: the basis for all of our human relationships is found in our relationship with the Lord. Before Paul even mentions the roles of husbands and wives, he instructs, "Therefore be imitators of God as dear children" (Eph. 5:1).

Your primary identity is not that of husband, wife, father, mother, man, or woman. Your primary identity is who you are in relationship to God: His dear child. As God's dear child, your most important responsibility is to invest in relationship with Him and obey Him. Ephesians 5:8 explains: "For you were once darkness, but now you are light in the Lord. Walk as children of light." When we cultivate relationship with God, He works through us to make our other relationships effective.

Real Love

Next, Paul instructs husbands to love their wives. The basic role of a husband toward his wife is simply this: loving cultivation. As we learned in an earlier chapter, Ephesians 5 and Colossians 3:19 tell husbands to love their wives: unconditionally, continually, sacrificially, affectionately, developmentally, and tenderly.

Question to Consider

One of the best gifts a man can give his kids is loving their mother. Look up the following Scriptures. How is a godly man to love his wife?

Ephesians 5:25 _____

_____

_____

Ephesians 5:28 _____

_____

_____

1 Peter 3:7 _____

_____

_____

Proverbs 5:18 _____

_____

_____

A Man and His Children

When my son Nathan was born and I held him in my arms for the first time, I remember feeling fear. I thought, "What if I drop him?" I also thought of Ephesians 6:4: "And you, fathers, do not provoke your children to wrath, but bring them up in the training and admonition of the Lord." Though the child in my arms was small and light, I was holding, for the first time, the full weight of the responsibility of being a dad. I asked myself, "What do I do with this child who will one day grow up?"

If you are a father, you have a relationship with your children. That relationship has parameters. In two verses of Scripture, God outlines those parameters: a negative command with an explanation, and a positive command. On the negative side we read, "Fathers, do not provoke your children, lest they become discouraged" (Col. 3:21). On the positive side, fathers are admonished to "bring them up in the training and admonition of the Lord" (Eph. 6:4).

Paul's instruction to fathers was a radical departure from the customs of the time in which Paul's letters were written. Under Roman law, a father could do anything he wanted with and to his children. When they were born, he could reject them. If he kept them, he could sell them as slaves or kill them if he chose. With that as a backdrop, Paul tells fathers not to provoke, but rather to nurture, care for, and direct their children's lives.

Do Not Provoke

First, let's examine the Bible's negative instruction to fathers: "do not provoke your children." Why does Paul address fathers this way? And why is this instruction addressed only to dads? Perhaps because Paul was in touch with human nature. As we've already studied, children do not naturally obey; yet what was Paul's instruction to them? "Children, obey your parents" (Eph. 6:1; Col. 3:20). Therefore, Paul may have chosen these words for fathers because fathers naturally provoke their children. While mothers tend to be more sensitive and nurturing, fathers are often goal-oriented and push their children to achieve and succeed.

What it Means

Let's look at what *provoke* means. *Erethizo*, the Greek word used in Colossians 3:21, means "to stir up, excite, stimulate, provoke." *Parorgizo*, the Greek term used in Ephesians 6:4, means "to rouse to wrath, to provoke, exasperate, anger." Other versions of the Bible translate this term "embitter" (NIV), "irritate" (AB), "exasperate" (NASB), "nag" (NCV), "vex" (YLT), "overcorrect" (Phillips), and "be hard on" (BBE). The Amplified Bible puts it this way: "Fathers, do not irritate or provoke your children to anger; do not exasperate them to resentment." These words indicate a process of behavior occurring over a long period of time that would build up resentment and discouragement within the heart of a child.

What it Looks Like

What are some ways fathers might provoke their children to wrath and discouragement?

• **Hypocrisy**

Saying one thing and doing another is a dangerous game. Kids have fine antennae. They hear and watch, and if things don't mesh, they start to wonder what is going on. Once they find out, their curiosity turns to disappointment, betrayal, and anger.

- **Criticism Without Compliment**

    If you criticize your child more often than you praise him or her, you are helping steer that child toward emotional trauma. As the child begins to grow up, he or she will lose hope, eventually becoming convinced he or she can't do anything right. Proverbs 15:1 tells us, "A soft answer turns away wrath, but a harsh word stirs up anger." I'm not saying take a back seat and don't help them excel; help them. Just remember, kids need lots of approval, encouragement, compassion, touch, and "I love you."

- **Poor Discipline**

    Many parents are inconsistent in the way they discipline their children. They respond one way to their child's behavior today, and in an entirely different manner tomorrow. Or Dad responds one way while Mom responds another.

    Inappropriate discipline can also harm a child. For example, let's say your child spills his milk and you fly off the handle. You launch into a verbal tirade, saying things without thinking and threatening punishment far more severe than the child's mistake merits. Once you have calmed down, you feel deeply ashamed. You may apologize to your child and quickly forget the words you said in anger, but those words form a deep emotional scar on your child's mind and heart.

    Some parents don't discipline at all. They say, "We'll let it go for now. Johnny was just having a bad day." Dare to love your child enough to discipline him or her fairly and consistently, keeping the same parameters.

- **Favoritism and Comparison**

    Comparing children with others, especially in front of siblings or friends, demeans them. I grew up in a goal-oriented family. My dad had certain goals for his boys. My brothers, for the most part, met those standards. As I grew up as number four, one of the most painful things I remember is my dad comparing one of us to the others. We also see examples of favoritism in Scripture. Joseph was favored by his father. Isaac favored Esau. Rebecca favored Jacob. That hurts—and the memory lasts. Give your children the right to be who they are, as they are.

- **Minimization or Disinterest**

    Fathers can provoke a child to wrath by making light of small problems that seem large to the child. For example, what happens when your child loses his teddy bear? You think, "What's a teddy bear in the scheme of life?" You say, "Don't worry about it; eat your breakfast." To a child, a lost teddy bear is big news. Don't minimize that. Try to get into your child's life and connect with how he or she is feeling. Respond to your child's thoughts and feelings rather than your own.

I came across a report a while back that just staggered me. It said the primary reason children go to foster homes today is not divorce, financial problems, or death of a parent. The greatest percentage of children in foster homes today are there because of disinterested parents.[39]

I also read about a speaker and researcher's experience with a church youth group. He asked forty-two junior and senior high kids, "Can you talk to your dad?" Only one said yes. Dads, aspire to be like the father of that one teen—like the father of the prodigal son in Jesus' parable. When the errant son finally came to his senses about the direction his life had taken, he said, "I will arise and go to my father, and will say to him, 'Father, I have sinned against heaven and before you'" (Luke 15:18). Happy is the child who can say, "I will go to my father." That child's father does not provoke his children.

- **Distrust and Control**

Part of good parenting is teaching and allowing children to make their own choices at appropriate times. Yes, they may fail, but failing is part of growing up. If they fail while still in your home, you have the opportunity to help them learn from their failure and grow their ability to make successful choices. When we do the opposite—ignore our children's opinions and make all their choices for them—we communicate that we don't trust them. Such distrust can create deep-seated resentment within the heart of a child and fails to equip them with the ability to make wise choices.

- **Selfishness**

Dads can also anger their children by failing to sacrifice for them. Too easily, dads can fill their time with work, sports, hobbies, trips, and chores. When dads do all these things without sacrificing for their children, their kids grow up believing they are the lowest priority in their father's life. They think, "You don't love me enough to sacrifice for me." True or not, this belief can definitely breed resentment, anger, wrath, and low self-worth in the heart of a child.

An early episode with my own son illustrates this point. I was studying for this chapter when Nathan interrupted me. He walked in and said, "Daddy, I have an owwie." After I kissed it he said, "My owwie goed away!" All he wanted was a little companionship—some of my time. As I looked at him, I thought: "I never want to be guilty of giving him everything he needs except the one thing he needs most: my time. I never want him to think, 'Dad was always busy. I know he said he loved me, but I never really saw it displayed.'"

WHY?

Why are fathers not to provoke their children? Colossians 3:21 tells us: "…lest they become discouraged." Other translations read, "… so that their spirit may not be broken" (BBE) and "they will become discouraged and quit trying" (NLT). *Athumeo*, the Greek term Paul uses, means "to be disheartened, dispirited, broken in spirit." Depending on a child's temperament and the relationship he or she has with his or her father, a father's criticism or constant encouragement to do better can harm both a child's self-esteem and the relationship between father and child.

Do you know what the plague of youth is? A broken spirit—sometimes broken by parents with high demands who never offer a word of encouragement. Parents, if you often tell your kids what they do wrong but never what they do right, they'll grow up with a crushed spirit. They may become adults who don't excel because they believe they are incapable of doing so, have little staying power, and are the first to give up when a challenge arises.

Here's what the Bible says about a broken spirit: "[A] broken spirit dries the bones" (Prov. 17:22) and "The spirit of a man will sustain him in sickness, but who can bear a broken spirit?" (Prov. 18:14). Fathers, I know this is not the legacy you want to give your children. Please don't provoke their sensitive spirits.

Ephesians 6:4 tells us children also respond to provocation with wrath. In other translations we find similar words: "anger" (NASB) and "resentment" (AB). Again, Scripture tells us the results wrath can produce: "A wrathful man stirs up strife…" (Prov. 15:18); "A man of great wrath will suffer punishment…" (Prov. 19:19); "As…wringing the nose produces blood, so the forcing of wrath produces strife" (Prov. 30:33); and "Wrath is cruel and anger a torrent…" (Prov. 27:4). Again, we see a picture of a future no father wants for his children.

BUILDER'S NOTES

Why are fathers not to provoke their children? Colossians 3:21 tells us: "…lest they become discouraged."

Questions to Consider

1. In a dictionary, look up the word *provoke* and write its definition below.

_____

_____

2. Consider the "don't" command of Ephesians 6:4. As a parent, do you "provoke your children to wrath"? Think of a specific time when your reaction to a problem might have hurt the heart of your child. Having read this section, how might you react to a similar situation if it occurred today?

_____

_____

_____

3. Dad, ask yourself the following questions regarding your discipline techniques.

Am I ever hypocritical or do I "practice what I preach"? _____

_____

Am I quick to blame? Do I balance my discipline with praise? _____

_____

Am I inconsistent, or do I apply the same discipline consistently? _____

_____

Am I ever unfair, or is my discipline fair to each child? _____

_____

Do I make unfair comparisons, or do I appreciate each child's abilities individually? _____

Do I make light of my child's problems, failing to take them seriously? Do I listen with my full attention when my child is trying to tell me something important to him or her? _____

_____

Do I allow my child to make decisions appropriate for his or her age level?

_____

Do I adequately sacrifice for my child? _____

_____

BLUEPRINTS

"You shall teach them diligently to your children, and shall talk of them when you sit in your house, when you walk by the way, when you lie down, and when you rise up."

Deut. 6:7

4. When your child asks you—directly or indirectly—for a little time and attention, do you view it as an interruption or an appointment? What is your response?

_____

_____

BRING THEM UP

On the positive side, Paul says, "But bring them up in the training and admonition of the Lord." Spiritual training of children is not Mom's responsibility, or the church's, or the Christian school's. Spiritual training is Dad's responsibility. Dads are the ones the Bible tells to "bring them up." Deuteronomy chapter 6 says fathers are to be the ones that infuse spiritual truths into the lives of their children: "You shall teach them diligently to your children, and shall talk of them when you sit in your house, when you walk by the way, when you lie down, and when you rise up" (Deut. 6:7). Admittedly, mothers who spend more time with the children during the day have more opportunity to do this than fathers who spend the workday away from home. However, fathers have many opportunities to, through precept and example, fulfill their biblical responsibilities to bring their children up "in the training and admonition of the Lord." Dads, a spiritual fiber should run through your family. Talk about Jesus at the dinner table and in conversations, in the morning and at night. Bring Jesus into everything you do with your kids.

Dads, a spiritual fiber should run through your family. Talk about Jesus at the dinner table and in conversations, in the morning and at night. Bring Jesus into everything you do with your kids.

BUILDER'S NOTES

I've had a great time with my son as he grows up. Almost every morning I get up, have a cup of coffee, get my Bible, and sit out in front. The sun's coming up, and it's a beautiful quiet time. As soon as Nathan wakes up, he comes outside. Nearly every morning, his first glimpse of me is me reading my Bible with a cup of coffee nearby. He usually asks, "Dad, can I have a cup of coffee?" Telling him, "Sure," I sit him down with a cup of "coffee" (doctored heavily with sugar and cream), open my Bible, and read him a Bible story. And we just sip coffee and talk about Jesus together early in the morning. It doesn't last long—his attention span is short—but it's quality time we share with God and each other nearly every day.

We've also developed a thing we call "Say, Play, and Pray." It's easy to say and easy to do. We read a Bible story together and then dress up as the characters. If it's Joshua in Jericho, I dress him up with a cotton beard, a little staff and a sword, give him a little trumpet to blow, and play the part of the people inside Jericho. When he blows the trumpet, I tumble the pillow walls down. After that, we pray about the spiritual lessons the story teaches us. He gets into bed with God's vibrant truth still tumbling around in his mind.

Saint Augustine was a very famous man of God. He wrote many works that greatly influenced the world during his time. In his book *Confessions*, he wrote this as a prayer to God:

No one had anything but praise for my father who, despite his slender resources, was ready to provide his son with all that was needed to enable him to travel so far for the purpose of study. Many of our townsmen, far richer than my father, went to no such trouble for their children's sake. Yet, the same father of mine took no trouble at all to see how I was growing in Your sight or whether I was chastised or not. He cared only that I should have a furtive tongue, leaving my heart to bear none of Your fruits, my God, though You are the only master true and good of its husbandry.[40]

Can you imagine having your son write that about you? "Yeah, Dad really worked hard to get me to college, but he never told me about Jesus. He never raised me up spiritually." I commend dads who work hard to provide for their families. I also caution you: don't forget you have a spiritual role to play as well.

I cannot emphasize enough the tremendous importance of strong spiritual leadership from the man of the house. I challenge each man to fulfill his God-given leadership role.

BUILDER'S NOTES

I cannot emphasize enough the tremendous importance of strong spiritual leadership from the man of the house. I challenge each man to fulfill his God-given leadership role.

Questions to Consider

1. Consider the positive command of Ephesians 6:4: "…bring them up in the training and admonition of the Lord." List three specific ways you can train and admonish your children in the Lord.

   1. _____

   2. _____

   3. _____

2. Fathers, examine the way you interact with your children and answer the following:

	Yes	No	Sometimes
Do I provoke my children?	❏	❏	❏
Do I give them biblical instruction?	❏	❏	❏
Do my actions back up my godly words?	❏	❏	❏
Do I encourage my children?	❏	❏	❏
Do I have reasonable goals for them?	❏	❏	❏
Do I tell them, "I love you"?	❏	❏	❏

3. If any of your answers to the previous question brought conviction to your heart, write a prayer to *your* Father, asking His forgiveness and dedicating yourself to being a servant father to your children.

   _____

   _____

   _____

4. Fathers, you are a role model of the Lord to your child. What will you begin to do today to guarantee you are the best possible role model for your son? For your daughter? _____

   _____

   _____

Mothers

SCULPTORS OF LIFE

M y hat goes off to moms for the tough job they do so well. It's rewarding, I
understand, but challenging nonetheless. Consider the hours a mom puts
in and the services she provides to her husband and children. If mothers were
to receive a wage, most husbands and children couldn't afford one! About
mothers, Theodore Roosevelt said:

> When all is said, it is the mother and the mother only who is a better
> citizen than the soldier who fights for his country. The successful
> mother, the mother who does her part in rearing and training aright the
> boys and girls who are to be the men and women of the next genera-
> tion, is of greater use to the community and occupies, if she would only
> realize it, a more honorable, as well as important, position than any
> man in it. The mother is the only one supreme asset of national life.
> She is more important by far than the successful statesmen or business-
> men or artists or scientists.[41]

Perhaps no statement about mothers is more true than this one: "The hand
that rocks the cradle is the hand that rules the world" (William Ross Wallace).
Scripture and history books are filled with women who influenced their children, husbands, communities, and world. I am convinced women are more
influential than any other group on earth, and a 2000 Gallup poll backs me up:

> Sorry, dads, but in spite of the sexual revolution, mothers still outscore
> fathers in the influence department—a finding that has changed little
> since Gallup first measured it nearly a half century ago. When asked to
> choose, a majority of Americans identify their mother, rather than their

BUILDER'S NOTES

The mother is the only one supreme asset of national life. She is more important by far than the successful statesmen or businessmen or artists or scientists.

—Theodore Roosevelt

father, as the one who had more influence on them when growing up, 53 percent vs. 28 percent.[42]

Numerous leaders have attributed their success to the influence of their mothers. President George Washington said, "All I am I owe to my mother. I attribute all my success in life to the moral, intellectual, and physical education I received from her." Similarly, President Abraham Lincoln said of his mother, "All that I am or ever hope to be, I owe to my angel Mother." Booker T. Washington paid this tribute: "If I have done anything in life worth attention, I feel sure that I inherited the disposition from my mother."

What about the rest of us? According to Gallup, nearly nine in ten American adults (88 percent) report that their own mother has had a positive influence on them. This includes 64 percent who say her influence has been "very positive" and another 24 percent who describe it as "somewhat positive."[43]

With this much influence, imagine the spiritual impact a *godly* mother can leverage in and through the lives of her children! In fact, Abraham Lincoln made the statement, "No man is poor who has a godly mother."

One of my favorite authors and teachers is G. Campbell Morgan. He and his wife had four sons, all of whom became ministers. Someone once asked Morgan and his sons, "Who's the best preacher in your family?" Together, they responded, "Mom." Morgan further added, "I got my dedication to the Scripture from my mother. I heard my first Bible stories from my mother."

Similarly, I heard a story about four scholars discussing which translation of the Bible was best. Unexpectedly, one scholar said, "I like my mom's translation the best." Laughing, the others joked, "Your mom translated the Bible, did she?" "Yes, she did," the student replied. "She translated every page of the Bible into her life, and it was the most convincing translation I've ever seen."

Women, if you aspire to be one thing, aspire to be a godly mother. I believe a woman's greatest potential is realized in motherhood. God's Word says the children of the godly woman "…rise up and call her blessed" (Prov. 31:28). Imagine what a different generation we would have today if all mothers saw babies in their wombs as eternal souls they have an opportunity to mold and shape, rather than mere pieces of flesh that can be disposed of prenatally. God gives mothers a unique opportunity. The church can teach Sunday School. Christian schools can stuff facts, figures, and certain things into children's minds. But only a parent can nurture and strengthen a child's faith for eternity by living and teaching that faith through the parent's own life, every minute of every day.

Questions to Consider

1. As we've read, many great leaders attribute much of their success to the influence of their mothers. How has your mother positively influenced your life? Write your thoughts below, and pray about making a commitment to tell your mother this week, if possible, how she has positively influenced your life. _____

   _____

   _____

   _____

2. General Andrew Jackson said about his mother, "Her teachings were, after all, the only capital I had to start life with, and on that capital I have made my way." Think about that powerful statement. What kind of capital are you providing your child upon which to build? Examine your heart, then answer the following questions.

	Yes	No	Sometimes
Are my words encouraging?	❑	❑	❑
Are my words edifying	❑	❑	❑
Are my words kind?	❑	❑	❑
Are my words gentle?	❑	❑	❑
Do my words honor the Lord?	❑	❑	❑

3. What "translation" of the Bible are you writing with your life? Will your children say, "My mother's/parent's version of the Bible was the most convicting version I have ever seen"?

   _____

   _____

MOMS IN SCRIPTURE

As we've noted before, God provides us with examples to follow for every role He calls us to fill. In this section, we'll look at godly characteristics demonstrated by four mothers in Scripture: the "virtuous wife" described in Proverbs 31; Hannah, wife of Elkanah and mother of Samuel; and Eunice and Lois, Timothy's mother and grandmother.

The Virtuous Wife

I came across the following paraphrase of Proverbs 31:10-31. Titled, "They Call Her Mother," it appeared in a newspaper several years ago.

Who can find a virtuous woman? For the value of her life is beyond monetary calculations. Her husband has absolute trust in her so that he has no need of satisfaction from other women. She will do him good and not evil all the days of her life. She keeps his clothing up to date, clean, and tidy. She willingly works around the house. She provides variety at mealtime by wise selection of nutritious and delicious foods. She gets up early each morning to make his breakfast and sees that the kids also eat properly. She knows a bargain when she sees one and is always concerned about future stability and supply of her home. The strength of her character is shown in her attitude toward the household tasks. She takes pride in a job well done, even if she has to work late hours to accomplish it. She knows how to use a sewing machine and needles. She has a compassionate heart and hand toward those who have great needs. Those in her home especially benefit from her domestic talents. Her own clothing shows good taste and modesty. Even her husband is known by her concern for his wearing apparel. She often uses her household talents to provide extra income for her family. She is known as a woman of honorable character. The humble expression of this character gives her an inner joy. She is wise in her speech and especially she knows how to say kind words. She's concerned about the interests and the problems of all in her house. She's not a gossip. Her children are happy to talk about her to their friends. Her husband also praises her to others. Other women have done great deeds, but this type of mother and wife ranks the highest. Popularity is deceitful, glamour is shallow, but a woman who has personal contact with the holy God, she shall be praised. She shall receive great satisfaction from her labors and others shall talk about her good deeds wherever they go.[44]

Wow—that's quite a woman! However, I'd like to clarify one thing: These character qualities and accomplishments are to be considered in the context of a lifetime—not 24 hours. I believe this passage presents a progression, referring to the entire career of a godly wife and mother.

Hannah

Hannah's claim to biblical fame is her role as mother and as a servant of the Lord. She had a problem: she was barren for many years of her marriage to Abraham. In a culture where children were literally the "pride and joy" of every Hebrew couple, and lack of children implied that a woman was cursed by God, this was a difficult burden for Hannah to bear. Yet, despite her difficulties, Hannah presents us with a portrait of a godly mother with godly priorities: devotion to God, devotion to her husband, devotion to prayer, and devotion to the children with which God blessed her as He promised.

Lois and Eunice

Christians tend to talk a lot about Paul and Timothy, friends and fellow ministers for Christ. We talk about how courageously and effectively they spread the Gospel, and their influence in strengthening the foundation of the church. Yet, how often do we talk about their mothers and grandmothers, those who labored behind the scenes to build the foundation without which Timothy may not have become the man Scripture describes?

The apostle Paul introduces us to Lois and Eunice. Writing to Timothy from a Roman prison at the end of his life, Paul says, "…I call to remembrance the genuine faith that is in you, which dwelt first in your grandmother Lois and your mother Eunice, and I am persuaded is in you also" (2 Tim. 1:5). In other words, "Timothy, when I think of you, I think of a person who has a genuine relationship with God. You got it from your mom, and she got it from her mom." Paul's words of encouragement to Timothy tell us some key things about the women who taught and nurtured Timothy in his youth, and the life-long impact of a godly mother's influence.

Questions to Consider

1. Proverbs 31:13-22 can be summed up in verse 27: "She watches over the ways of her household, and does not eat the bread of idleness." Read verses 13-22, viewing them as a progression throughout a woman's life. Which tasks could be accomplished when children are small? Which are more easily undertaken when children have grown and have left home?

_____

_____

2. Look up the following Scripture references. In addition to Hannah, what other women of the Bible had "closed wombs"?

Genesis 11:29-30 – S _____

Genesis 25:21 – R _____

Genesis 29:31 – R _____

Judges 13:2-24 – M_____'s wife; the mother of S _____

2 Samuel 6:20-23 – M _____

Luke 1:5-7 – E _____

3. Some elements of society claim Christianity diminishes the role of women. On the contrary, Christianity elevates a woman's position. Read the following Scriptures, name each woman mentioned, and briefly describe her influence on her world.

Scripture	Name	Influence
Acts 9:36		
Acts 16:14-15		
Romans 16:3-4		

Relationship with God

Being a godly mother begins with a relationship with God. When we dedicate children at Calvary of Albuquerque we pray for the parents. In fact, we make sure parents are dedicated to the Lord before we dedicate their children. Many times parents will say to the church, "Train up my child in the way of the Lord. I don't want to get involved, but I know they need a Christian education." Parents, you can't expect your child to know and grow in the Lord unless you know Him first. A mother must nourish her own soul before she can nourish the souls of her children.

Love for God

Do you remember the lawyer who asked Jesus, "Which is the first commandment of all" (Mark 12:28)? Jesus answered, "You shall love the Lord your God with all your heart, with all your soul, with all your mind, and with all your strength…" (Mark 12:30). Moms are no exception. Being a godly mother first requires loving God with all of your heart, mind, soul, and strength.

Hannah was a woman in right relationship with God. When the son for whom she had prayed was born, she prayed a passionate prayer of specific praise to and love for her Lord (1 Sam. 2:1-10). Her prayer begins with the words: "[M]y heart rejoices in the LORD; my horn is exalted in the LORD. I smile at my enemies, because I rejoice in Your salvation. No one is holy like the LORD, for there is none besides You, nor is there any rock like our God" (1 Sam. 2:1-2). Hannah knew and loved God.

Questions to Consider

1. One important characteristic of a loving, effective mother is godliness. *Godliness* means having "piety or reverence toward God." Godliness means more than religious profession and a godly conduct; it also means the reality and power of a vital union with God."[45] Read 1 Timothy 2:1-3.

2. In verses 1 and 2, for whom does Paul exhort us to pray? _____

   _____

3. We are to pray for those who are in authority in order to lead what kind of lives? _____

   _____

BUILDER'S NOTES

Being a godly mother first requires loving God with all of your heart, mind, soul, and strength.

4. According to verse 3, why are we to lead lives "in godliness and reverence"?

_____

5. How important is your relationship with the Lord? Do you love Him above all others? Do you make Him your first priority? Read the following and mark all that apply.

I make God a priority in my life by:

❑ Reading His Word daily
❑ Spending time alone with Him
❑ Meditating on His Word day and night
❑ Praying at all times
❑ Worshiping Him with song and praise
❑ Sharing with others what He has done for me
❑ Sharing in communion
❑ Other:

6. In 1 Samuel 2:1-2, Hannah prays to the Lord:
"My heart rejoices in the Lord …
I smile at my enemies …
I rejoice in Your salvation.
No one is holy like the Lord …
Nor is there any rock like our God."

BUILDER'S NOTES

Becoming and being a godly mother requires time with God. A mother needs strength and support from God to weather the storms of mothering.

7. Following Hannah's example, pen your own prayer to the Father:

_____

_____

_____

_____

_____

Time with God

Becoming and being a godly mother requires time with God. I understand moms have little time to themselves, but I can't emphasize enough the importance of making and taking that time. A mother needs strength and support from God to weather the storms of mothering. It's too difficult a job to do alone. To be a godly mother who gives her children her best, a mother must first be committed to the Lord and experience the strength of the Holy Spirit working through her. It's during the quiet times of stillness and connection that God shapes a woman's convictions and gives her strength and wisdom for her role as a mother.

BLUEPRINTS 📖

"Be anxious for nothing, but in everything by prayer and supplication, with thanksgiving, let your requests be made known to God; and the peace of God, which surpasses all understanding, will guard your hearts and minds through Christ Jesus."

Phil. 4:6-7

Pouring Out Her Soul

Hannah spent time with God. Every year she accompanied her husband to Shiloh to worship and sacrifice to the Lord (1 Sam. 1:3-7). But Hannah's relationship with God was more than a yearly ritual. In 1 Samuel 1, we see her fast instead of feast and go to the tabernacle to "pour out her soul before the Lord" (1 Sam. 1:15). What a wonderful definition of prayer.

Prayer is a window of the heart, a looking-glass into the soul. You learn a lot about a person when you hear them pray. I'll never forget my first date with Lenya. We went to her father's house after the date and I sat with her and said, "Let's pray." Just a few weeks old in the Lord, she told me, "I don't know how to pray," and she didn't pray that evening. A couple of years later, at the end of another date, we prayed together again. This time she prayed, and I fell in love with her as I listened in on her relationship with God. I realized how much she had grown as a Christian, and that her relationship with God had gone far deeper than mine.

Today, when people tell me, "I don't know how to pray," I ask them, "Do you know how to talk?" Just talk to God. That's prayer! Whatever is on your heart, pour it out. He's listening. All your hurts and needs (and moms have lots of them)—anxieties, ambitions, and emotions—pour them out to the Lord. Scripture says: "Cast your burden on the LORD, and He shall sustain you…" (Ps. 55:22) and "[H]umble yourselves under the mighty hand of God, that He may exalt you in due time, casting all your care upon Him, for He cares for you" (1 Pet. 5:6-7).

Mothers, pray for your children. Commit them to the Lord. When you pray, pray in faith—then let go. God's hands are the safest place children can be.

Receiving God's Peace

In addition to being a venue for pouring out one's soul to the Lord, prayer is also a source of peace. The Bible gives us this command with a promise: "Be anxious for nothing, but in everything by prayer and supplication, with thanksgiving, let your requests be made known to God; and the peace of God, which surpasses all understanding, will guard your hearts and minds through Christ Jesus" (Phil. 4:6-7).

In faith, Hannah made a vow that if God granted her a son, she would "…give him to the LORD all the days of his life…" (1 Sam. 1:11). After observing her prayer and talking with her, the priest Eli told Hannah, "…Go in peace, and the God of Israel grant your petition which you have asked of Him" (1 Sam. 1:17). Having prayed her prayer with confidence and received God's peace through Eli's blessing, Hannah—who had been weeping and too sad to eat— "…went her way and ate, and her face was no longer sad" (1 Sam. 1:18). She had committed her request to the Lord and left it in His hands.

Hannah also received God's peace through prayer when she kept her vow to God. In 1 Samuel we read her prayers when she and her husband took Samuel to the tabernacle to begin his career of serving God: "For this child I prayed, and the LORD has granted me my petition which I asked of Him. Therefore I also have lent him to the LORD; as long as he lives he shall be lent to the LORD …He will guard the feet of His saints…He will give strength to His king, and exalt the horn of His anointed" (1 Sam. 1:27-28; 2:9-10). Hannah knew God had given her Samuel. She knew God was the source of the strength and peace she needed to keep her vow to Him. And she knew God would be with both mother and son while they were apart.

Praying God's Praise

Godly mothers give God the praise He deserves. As they spend time with Him and as they serve their families, godly mothers realize more and more how dependent on God they are for their success as mothers. As God faithfully provides them with all they need, they give the praise to Him.

Hannah models this beautifully. Even when she was parting with her son at a very young age, the Bible tells us, "[T]hey worshiped the LORD there" (1 Sam. 1:28). And then Hannah prayed a prayer of praise exalting God's faithfulness, generosity, justice, and power.

Fulfilling God's Purpose

There's a secret about prayer in Hannah's story: Hannah's barrenness was God's divine design. In 1 Samuel 1:5-6, we read not once, but twice: "the LORD closed her womb." God did it on purpose. Why? Scripture shows us Hannah's childlessness drove her to the Lord. Only God could change her situation, and she knew it. So she bargained with God, asking for a son, and promising to give that son back to God for his entire lifetime. That was God's plan from the beginning: to raise up Samuel as a prophet to turn the nation of Israel from its apostasy and back to God.

God used Hannah's situation to cause her to cry out to Him, and in doing so, align herself with His purposes. Once she was aligned with God's will, He told her, "You're on; it'll happen." That's the purpose of prayer. Prayer is not about getting our will done in heaven; it's about letting God align our hearts with His purposes, so He can then do through us what He intended to do from the beginning. In Hannah's case, God used a godly mother to turn a nation back to Him.

Questions to Consider

1. Moms, in order to weather the storms of mothering, you need the strength and support God freely gives. According to the following Scriptures, what resources are available to believers to weather life's storms?

Mark 14:38 _____

BUILDER'S NOTES

Godly mothers give God the praise He deserves. As they spend time with Him and as they serve their families, godly mothers realize more and more how dependent on God they are for their success as mothers.

John 14:16-17 _____

Hebrews 4:12 _____

James 1:5-6 _____

2. Part of a vital union with God is a strong prayer life. We lead godly lives before our children when we demonstrate the importance of prayer in our lives. What do the following Scriptures say about prayer?

1 Samuel 12:23 _____

Psalm 55:17 _____

Matthew 26:41 _____

Mark 11:25 _____

Luke 6:28 _____

Luke 18:1 _____

Luke 22:40 _____

1 Corinthians 14:15 _____

1 Thessalonians 5:17 _____

3. Prayer is described above as "a window of the heart" and "a looking-glass into the soul." Take a moment to write your own description of prayer.

Prayer is _____

_____

_____

4. Do you pray for your children every day? Read Philippians 4:6-7, then write a prayer entrusting your children to God and claiming the peace He offers.

_____

_____

_____

5. The purpose of prayer is to align our will with God's will. How are we *not* to pray? When will our prayers *not* be answered? Examine these two questions in the following Scriptures.

I am *not* to pray:

James 1:6-8 _____

Matthew 6:5-6 _____

Matthew 6:7 _____

God will *not* hear me when:

Psalm 66:18 _____

Isaiah 59:2 _____

1 John 5:14 _____

Genuine Faith

Timothy received from his mother and grandmother a heritage of genuine faith.
Paul's letter to Timothy reads, "I call to remembrance the genuine faith that is
in you, which dwelt first in your grandmother Lois and your mother Eunice,
and I am persuaded is in you also" (2 Tim. 1:5). Paul knew Timothy's spiritual
roots were from the maternal side of his family:

> *Then [Paul] came to Derbe and Lystra. And behold, a certain disciple was
> there, named Timothy, the son of a certain Jewish woman who believed, but
> his father was Greek. He was well spoken of by the brethren who were at
> Lystra and Iconium. Paul wanted to have him go on with him. And he
> took him and circumcised him because of the Jews who were in that region,
> for they all knew that his father was Greek. And as they went through the
> cities, they delivered to them the decrees to keep, which were determined by
> the apostles and elders at Jerusalem. So the churches were strengthened in
> the faith, and increased in number daily.* Acts 16:1-5

Many scholars believe that when Paul came to Derbe and Lystra the first
time, two of his many converts were Lois and Eunice, who grew up Jewish,
heard about the Messiah and believed Jesus was the Messiah. As their faith
grew, they led Timothy to Christ. When Paul returned, Timothy was maturing
as a believer and gaining a reputation as a spiritual young man. As a result, Paul
invited Timothy to travel with him.

Notice the word *genuine* in 2 Timothy 1:5. It is translated from the Greek
word *anupokritos*, which means "without hypocrisy." In Paul's time, the term
hypocrite referred to a stage actor who played a role in a performance. Paul uses
this term to say, "You live your Christian life genuinely, Timothy, without a
mask. I know you received this ability from your mother and grandmother,
whose faith is the same genuine faith I see in you."

I love Paul's description of Timothy's mother: "...a Jewish woman who
believed." A woman who believes in God possesses immeasurable power—
power that comes from her relationship with the Lord of the universe, and the
power to pass that faith to the next generation.

📖 BLUEPRINTS

"I call to remembrance the genuine faith that is in you, which dwelt first in your grandmother Lois and your mother Eunice, and I am persuaded is in you also."
2 Tim. 1:5

BUILDER'S NOTES

When a child knows Mom and Dad are madly in love with each other, he or she feels secure. Love God and love each other.

Questions to Consider

1. A godly person is one whose life is lived in the Spirit, by the Spirit, and shows evidence of the fruits of the Spirit. Read Galatians 5:22-23 and list the nine fruits of the Spirit listed.

   1. _____   6. _____

   2. _____   7. _____

   3. _____   8. _____

   4. _____   9. _____

   5. _____

2. Is a particular "fruit" missing from your life or that the Lord desires to see manifested more fully in your life? If so, write its name here:_____

3. Using a concordance, find three Scriptures that describe the particular fruit you listed above and write the references below. Choose one to memorize this week.

   _____

   _____

4. Timothy's faith was found first in his grandmother and in his mother. In order to have godly children, moms must themselves be godly. They must have a close personal relationship with God in order to teach their children to have such a relationship. Based on the following Scriptures, complete these sentences:

   Psalm 119:66: I believe _____

   Jeremiah 26:13: I will obey _____

   Psalm 37:3: I will trust _____

   Mark 11:22: I will have faith _____

Devotion to Her Husband

Secondly, a godly mother cultivates a right relationship with her husband. As I've mentioned before, I believe the greatest two things parents can do for their children are: love God with all of their hearts and declare it openly, and demonstrate their love for each other as husband and wife. Cultivated with commitment, this dynamic combination can overcome any challenge and impact children's lives positively throughout their lifetimes.

When a child knows Mom and Dad are madly in love with each other, he or she feels secure; when this love is absent (or the evidence of it is not present), a child becomes insecure. In turn, statistics show this insecurity becomes manifested in that child's life in a variety of negative ways. Love God and love each other.

Questions to Consider

1. If a stranger asked your children, "Are your mom and dad in love with each other?" what would their response most likely be?

   _____

   _____

2. Read Matthew 22:37-39 and answer the following:

   What is the first and great commandment? _____

   _____

   What is the second commandment?   _____

   _____

   Who is your closest "neighbor"? _____

   _____

3. Just as we are not to be "undercover Christians"—Christians who never declare their love for Jesus Christ—neither should we be hesitant to declare openly our love for our spouses. Declare your love for the Lord and for one another frequently!

Devotion To Her Children

Third, a godly mother is sacrificially committed to her children. She sees her children as a heritage from God—a wonderful privilege, a worthy calling and a responsibility deserving nothing less than her best.

Time

British psychiatrist John Bowlby said, "The young child's hunger for his mother's love and her presence is as great as his hunger for food. Her absence inevitably generates a powerful sense of loss and anger."

We read in 1 Samuel 1 that Hannah chose to spend as much time with Samuel as she could and gave up other opportunities so she could do so.

Now the man Elkanah and all his house went up to offer to the LORD the yearly sacrifice and his vow. But Hannah did not go up, for she said to her husband, "Not until the child is weaned; then I will take him, that he may appear before the LORD and remain there forever." ...Then the woman stayed and nursed her son until she had weaned him. 1 Sam. 1:21-23

 **BUILDER'S NOTES**

A godly mother is sacrificially committed to her children. She sees her children as a heritage from God—a wonderful privilege, a worthy calling and a responsibility deserving nothing less than her best.

Many women would jump at a chance to get away—at least for a little while—from staying at home with a young child. Vacation at Shiloh, lay in the sun, take a break. In fact, it's good for parents to make time to get away together—both with and without the children. But Hannah's situation was different because she knew she had only three years with Samuel—the length of time women of her day took to wean their children. Hannah had dedicated her son to the Lord, and would leave him at the tabernacle in Shiloh three years after his birth. Because she wanted to be an influence in his life, she decided to stay with Samuel rather than go to the annual feast.

BUILDER'S NOTES

Charles Spurgeon used to say, "Before a child reaches seven, teach him all the way to heaven. And better still the work will thrive if he learns it before he's five."

Questions to Consider

1. Look up the word *devote* in a dictionary and record the definition below.

   _____

   _____

2. To whom are you devoted?
   ❑ To my Lord   ❑ To my spouse   ❑ To my child(ren)

Teaching and Training

Do you know a child's first five years of development are the most important? Eighty-five percent of a child's character is developed before age five. Charles Spurgeon used to say, "Before a child reaches seven, teach him all the way to heaven. And better still the work will thrive if he learns it before he's five."

One night before bed, Nathan said to me, "Dad, listen to this. Godliness with contentment is great gain." I asked, "Nathan, do you know what that means?" He started explaining the text to me, giving me a little Bible study. When he had finished, I told him, "Nathan, that's great. Where did you learn that?" He said, "Mom."

As used in 1 Samuel chapter 1, the term *weaned* means "to deal fully with."[46] In other words, Hannah told her husband, "I am going to deal fully with my son Samuel." To me, this states a strong case for moms and dads to devote themselves early to their children's spiritual development, rather than relying on other sources. Hannah knew she would take Samuel to the tabernacle where he would receive more spiritual training that his parents could likely provide on their own. Nonetheless, Hannah took seriously her opportunity and responsibility to teach her young son what she knew while he was with her.

Paul also showed us two godly mothers who passed God's truth from one generation to another. Speaking to Timothy he says, "You must continue in the things which you have learned and been assured of, knowing from whom you have learned them, and that from childhood you have known the Holy Scriptures, which are able to make you wise for salvation through faith which is in Christ Jesus" (2 Tim. 3:14-15). Paul isn't referring to himself as the one "from whom you have learned"; he's speaking of Timothy's mother and grandmother. Timothy had Lois and Eunice teaching him the truth from an early age.

In Deuteronomy 6, God gave Israel the law to obey. Then He said, "You shall teach them diligently to your children, and shall talk of them when you sit in your house, when you walk by the way, when you lie down, and when you rise up" (Deut. 6:7). In essence, the Word of God should be part of everything you do—even daily tasks like setting the breakfast table, getting ready for work, or watering the lawn. This is the model a godly mother provides for her children.

Questions to Consider

1. Mothers, do you read the Bible to your children, or let your children read it to you? Many excellent Bibles and books are geared to a child's level of understanding. How have you incorporated Bible study into your child's life? If you haven't yet begun, what first step can you take to begin now?

2. Moms, do your children see you make time to spend alone with God each day?

3. How do they see your love for God in the things you do throughout the day?

4. Husbands, does your wife need your help to find time for her to spend alone with God daily? How can you help?

5. Look up 1 Samuel 2:26. In what two things did Samuel grow?

   Mothers, what more could you desire for your child than to have them grow in these two things?

Tenderness

The word *tender* is defined as "marked by, responding to, or expressing the softer emotions; showing care." Most of us—though I know there are exceptions—learned tenderness from Mom and firmness from Dad. My father had moments of tenderness but my mom had a lifestyle of tenderness. I remember my dad saying, "Good job, son, but I know you can do better. Let me help you." I'm glad he encouraged me to grow and volunteered to come alongside. But it was my mom who put her arm around me and said, "You did great. I love you just the way you are."

Similarly, I remember seeing my dad cry some, but I remember seeing my mother cry more. It's the same way in my home today. Nathan has seen me cry, but not often. He has seen my wife cry much more because she's a tender mother. She possesses the attribute of tenderness, and expresses it. Moms, one of your greatest contributions to your family is the tenderness you display. I believe tenderness is a wonderful trait for young children to observe and learn.

Paul tells us Timothy possessed the characteristic of tenderness. In his second letter to Timothy, Paul says, "...being mindful of your tears..." likely referring to emotions Timothy had previously expressed in Paul's presence (2 Tim. 1:4). The first thing Paul remembered as he thought of Timothy while sitting in a Roman prison was Timothy's tears.

I believe Timothy had his mother to thank for his ability to display tenderness. The Bible tells us Timothy was "...the son of a certain Jewish woman who believed, but his father was Greek" (Acts 16:1). Many believe Timothy's father died while he was young, and he was raised by his mother and his grandmother. In this feminine environment, he learned the sort of tenderness he displayed in front of Paul.

Tenderness is also an attribute of godliness. Though God is called "Father" throughout Scripture, He models the motherly quality of tenderness. For example, God promised Israel, "As one whom his mother comforts, so I will comfort you; and you shall be comforted in Jerusalem" (Isa. 66:13). God also told His people, "Can a woman forget her nursing child, and not have compassion on the son of her womb? Surely they may forget, yet I will not forget you" (Isa. 49:15).

Paul also uses maternal comparison to express godly tenderness. Speaking of himself and Timothy, Paul wrote to the Thessalonians, "But we were gentle among you, just as a nursing mother cherishes her own children" (1 Thes. 2:7).

Questions to Consider

1. One characteristic of a godly mother is tenderness. In 2 Timothy 1:4, Paul remembered Timothy's demonstration of tenderness: "...being mindful of your tears ...," which he had most likely learned from his mother. How does your family react to tears? Does each member of your household believe it is okay to cry?

_____

_____

BLUEPRINTS

As one whom his mother comforts, so I will comfort you; and you shall be comforted in Jerusalem.
(Isa. 66:13)

2. In the Scriptures, God demonstrates tenderness toward us repeatedly, often in the form of comfort. Read the following and list the ways your heavenly Father stands ready to comfort His children.

Isaiah 66:13 _____

2 Corinthians 1:3-4 _____

2 Corinthians 7:6 _____

2 Thessalonians 2:16-17 _____

3. Read the following attributes of a tender person. Which can be used to describe you?

❑ Gentle ❑ Affectionate ❑ Patient
❑ Kindhearted ❑ Sweet-spirited ❑ Thoughtful

4. Choose one attribute listed above that you desire to be more evident in your life. Using a concordance, find a Scripture that speaks of this attribute and write it below. Determine today to begin demonstrating this attribute to your family. Ask the Lord to equip you to do this.

_____

_____

5. First Peter 3:8-9 says, "Finally, all of you be of one mind, having compassion for one another; love as brothers, be tenderhearted, be courteous; not returning evil for evil or reviling for reviling, but on the contrary blessing, knowing that you were called to this, that you may inherit a blessing." In your own words, describe what it means to be *tenderhearted*. Can you think of one example from Scripture where Jesus demonstrated tenderheartedness?

_____

_____

6. A mother's love has been described many different ways. Mothers, ask yourself the following questions:

	Always	Sometimes	Never
Am I protective?	❑	❑	❑
Am I tender?	❑	❑	❑
Is my love consistent?	❑	❑	❑
Do I try to be understanding?	❑	❑	❑
Am I quick to forgive?	❑	❑	❑
Is my love unselfish?	❑	❑	❑
Is my love comfortable?	❑	❑	❑

Tasks

A godly mother expresses her love and fulfills her role through the tasks she performs for her family. While raising young children, the virtuous woman described in Proverbs 31 shops, works with her hands, and provides food and clothing for her family and others (Prov. 31:13-15, 19-22, 27).

Hannah, too, made clothing for her son even though she was apart from him: "[Samuel's] mother used to make him a little robe, and bring it to him year by year when she came up with her husband to offer the yearly sacrifice" (1 Sam. 2:19).

Sacrifice

Sadly, many of us don't have to look far to find a parent or parents pursuing career or other passions while forfeiting relationship with their young children. Why? They're unwilling to sacrifice. Parenting requires sacrifice. Kids take up time and space in your life, which means some of the things that occupied that time and space before must be sacrificed.

Hannah made the ultimate sacrifice: she physically gave her son to the Lord. Unlike many of today's mothers, she didn't give her son away because she had been sexually irresponsible or because she simply didn't have room in her life to be a parent. She gave her son into God's service because she had made a promise and because that promise was part of God's plan.

Before she became pregnant, Hannah made an irrevocable commitment to give her first son to God "all the days of his life" (1 Sam. 1:11). Moms, can you imagine? She wanted a child more than anything, yet she was willing to give him back to God in exchange for the privilege of bringing him into the world, spending only the first few years with him, and being his mom from a distance for the rest of his life.

After Samuel's birth, she reaffirmed to her husband her intention to keep her vow: "[T]hen I will take him, that he may appear before the LORD and remain there forever" (1 Sam. 1:22). For the first three years of Samuel's young life, Hannah made sacrifices to devote as much time as she could to her son. Then, after weaning Samuel, she kept her commitment to God: "I also have lent him to the LORD; as long as he lives he shall be lent to the LORD" (1 Sam. 1:28). Because she made a promise to God, and because God gave her a son, Hannah sacrificed.

I remember the early years of marriage before children—years of freedom and quiet. I could come home from work, sit down, take off my shoes, and enjoy the aroma of dinner wafting through the house. Now when I come through the door, I have to duck! Nathan's playing dinosaur or soldier or something new everyday. His bedroom looks like a toy store after a tornado. If I think I've sacrificed some of home's calmer comforts, Lenya has sacrificed a thousand times more. Yet, both of us agree: our sacrifices are well worth their cost. We've made an investment in our son, and we're adding to it every day. We're confident its return will be far greater than the sacrifices we've made along the way.

Questions to Consider

1. What does it mean to be "sacrificially committed" to your family? In what ways was Hannah sacrificially committed?

_____

_____

_____

2. According to your description above, are you a sacrificially committed parent?

_____

_____

_____

Rewards

What are the results of godly mothering? The Bible tells us children, themselves, are a reward from God: "Children are a heritage from the LORD, the fruit of the womb is a reward" (Ps. 127:3). Psalm 17 tells us children bring satisfaction: "They are satisfied with children…" (Ps. 17:14).

One of Hannah's rewards for being a godly mother and keeping her vow to God was more children: "And Eli would bless Elkanah and his wife, and say, 'The LORD give you descendants from this woman for the loan that was given to the LORD.' …And the LORD visited Hannah, so that she conceived and bore three sons and two daughters" (1 Sam. 2:20-21). (A word to those who already have all the young "rewards" they can handle: Don't worry; God has *many* diverse and creative ways of rewarding those who faithfully serve Him.)

As we have mentioned previously, Proverbs 31 tells us the godly mother receives the reward of recognition and praise from her family: "Her children rise up and call her blessed; her husband also, and he praises her" (Prov. 31:28). In addition, she is promised joy: "…she shall rejoice in time to come" (Prov. 31:25).

Most importantly, I think we find the godly mom's greatest reward and blessing in 1 Sam. 2:21 and 2:26. "Meanwhile the child Samuel grew before the LORD…And the child Samuel grew in stature, and in favor both with the LORD and men." The godly efforts of Lois and Eunice were also rewarded. Timothy grew to become a man about whom Paul would say, "…when I call to remembrance the genuine faith that is in you, which dwelt first in your grandmother

BLUEPRINTS

"Children are a heritage from the LORD, the fruit of the womb is a reward" (Ps. 127:3). Psalm 17 tells us children bring satisfaction: "They are satisfied with children…" Ps. 17:14

BUILDER'S NOTES

She patrols the streets, stops a fight in the backyard, catches a tennis ball before it is flushed down the toilet, prevents a child from falling out of a tree, and moves the toys out of the driveway before Dad comes home, all at the same time.

Lois and your mother Eunice, and I am persuaded is in you also. Therefore I remind you to stir up the gift of God which is in you..."
(2 Tim. 1:5-6).

Now that's rewarding, isn't it? There won't be any greater joy for me than my child or children getting to know God personally and serving Him with all of their hearts. I don't care if they become a doctor or a lawyer or anything else. I just want them to love and serve Jesus Christ with their hearts and lives in "genuine faith." If you have one overwhelming desire for your child's life, I hope and pray it is for your child to fall in love with Jesus and live for Him.

Women, the position of mother is the most influential you could occupy in this world. With that in mind, do it with all of your heart. The following is a description of a world-class mother:

A mother appears to be a normal human being. She has all the physical features that all people have: two eyes, two hands, two arms, two feet, all connected to one body. Now, that's what you see if you just look at the exterior of a mother. But if you were a child, you know that she has at least three sets of eyes. Two in front, two in back, so that she can see all the things that she must see but that are hidden from her, and one on each side of her head so that she can protect the cookie jar no matter where she stands in the kitchen. All of these eyes are capable of seeing through wood, plaster, and so forth so she can tell what's going on behind closed doors. And she has bionic ears. She can hear a dirty word whispered a block away. She can hear a complaint that is only thought when unpleasant tasks are assigned to her kids. With her many arms and hands, she can prepare a meal, find Dad's shirt, change a diaper, run the vacuum, and hug two kids all at the same time. With strong, fast legs, she can move about the house like a speeding bullet. She patrols the streets, stops a fight in the backyard, catches a tennis ball before it is flushed down the toilet, prevents a child from falling out of a tree, and moves the toys out of the driveway before Dad comes home, all at the same time. Her endless supply of energy can only be a God-given attribute. She's the first to rise in the morning, have breakfast ready for the brood as they get up, gets each child ready for school, is both barber and beautician, fashion consultant, chairman, budget director, purchasing agent, paramedic, veterinarian, interpreter, travel agent, interior decorator, and is the last to bed at night. With a tender kiss, she can heal everything from a cut finger to a broken heart. With her kiss, she can convince a balding 40-year-old man that he's just as handsome as ever. Her ability to love is exceeded only by God's love. Her love is protective. Her love is tender. Her love is consistent and understanding, forgiving, unchanging, unselfish, giving, contagious, comfortable, and everlasting. The nearest thing that we can see in this world to God's love is a mother's love.[47]

Stay at it, moms! I salute you.

Questions to Consider

1. In Psalm 127:3, children are described as being "…a heritage from the Lord." Look up the word *heritage* in a dictionary and write its definition below.

   _____

   _____

2. From whom do we inherit our children? _____

3. Psalm 127:3 also says children are a "reward." When was the last time you thought of your children as being a reward? Write a prayer thanking God for the reward(s) He has given you in your children.

   _____

   _____

   _____

Parents

GOD'S PARTNERS

I was raised in what I consider an average American home. The youngest of four boys, I experienced the typical rebellion most kids and teens go through. I remember looking at my parents and thinking, "You've got an easy job. You get to boss your kids around. They do the chores for you. What a breeze." I also remember thinking, "I'm never going to be like they are."

Then I became a parent. As Henry Ward Beecher aptly said, "We never know the love of a parent till we become parents ourselves." When you become a parent, your attitudes about parenting, and perhaps toward your own parents, change overnight. You find yourself parenting your child in some of the exact ways you swore you never would.

I think parenting may be the toughest occupation and ministry on earth to do well. Few of us had classes in college or elsewhere on how to be a parent. For the most part, parenting is on-the-job training. By the time you're experienced, you're unemployed. Your kids are on their own in the big wide world, and you pray every day that you did your job right.

Parenting may also be the greatest privilege God gives human beings: the ability to create life, and the opportunity and responsibility to nurture that life into a life that glorifies God. Not a job to be taken lightly, parenting is an honor and awesome responsibility.

No one has parenting perfected. The Bible includes numerous examples of parents who got it very wrong. We can read every parenting book ever published and try our hardest not to make mistakes, but there is no such thing on earth as a perfect parent. For all of us, parenting is an adventure of learning, making mistakes, getting tired, and being rewarded along the way. Whatever your situation today, this is an important chapter for you.

BUILDER'S NOTES

Family values are changing rapidly and constantly. To many, the word obey and the phrase "obey your parents" are old-fashioned and outdated.

Questions to Consider

1. Do you agree or disagree that parenting "may be the toughest occupation and ministry on earth to do well?" If you agree, what are some of the reasons parenting can be so tough? _____

_____

_____

2. Parenting can also be rewarding. What have been some of your rewards as a parent?

_____

_____

RIGHTS AND ROLES

Parents and Children

Family values are changing rapidly and constantly. To many, the word *obey* and the phrase "obey your parents" are old-fashioned and outdated. As a society, we've fallen so far from God's design that 1977 was called the International Year of the Child. People convened from all over the world to declare the rights of children, liberate children from their homes, and make them wards of the state so parents couldn't teach them values. In some countries, there's a push to allow children sexual freedom. There's a viewpoint that supports children receiving minimum wage for doing household chores. Others even believe children should have the right to choose their own families.

At the other end of the spectrum are those who believe children have no rights, no feelings, and little value. I remember reading a magazine article that featured a picture of a man dangling a child in mid-air. The caption read, "He's got the whole world in his hands." Apparently, after a family quarrel, the man in the photo took his four-month-old baby to his apartment window and threatened to drop her to her death thirty feet below. Fortunately police nabbed him just in time and a fireman saved the child. That's our society, folks. Through divorce, absentee and inattentive parenting, irresponsible sexual activity, and more, a large part of our society sends the message every day that children are mere possessions to be ignored, passed around, created, or abandoned.

Then there's the Bible's view. The New Testament instructs, "Children, obey your parents..." (Eph. 6:1; Col. 3:20). To parents, Solomon says, "Train up a child in the way he should go, and when he is old he will not depart from it" (Prov. 22:6); and "Correct your son, and he will give you rest; yes, he will give delight to your soul" (Prov. 29:17).

What do you believe? Paul tells us, "[D]o not be conformed to this world, but be transformed by the renewing of your mind, that you may prove what is that good and acceptable and perfect will of God" (Rom. 12:2). I challenge you as Joshua boldly challenged Israel: "Choose for yourselves this day whom you will serve. ...As for me and my house, we will serve the LORD" (Josh. 24:15).

Parents and God

As discussed earlier, children are God's creations, entrusted to parents for all they need to grow and thrive. Someone once described the relationship between parents and God this way: "Parents are partners with God in discipling their children." Parents are children's caretakers and teachers, appointed by God and accountable to Him for their performance in this role. Jesus told His disciples, "For everyone to whom much is given, from him much will be required; and to whom much has been committed, of him they will ask the more" (Luke 12:48). Jesus also said, "Whoever causes one of these little ones who believe in Me to sin, it would be better for him if a millstone were hung around his neck, and he were drowned in the depth of the sea" (Matt. 18:6).

God's standard is much higher than the world's, and as such, more difficult to attain. However, every time God sets a standard, He gives us the ability to meet it through the power He gives us. Peter tells us, "...His divine power has given to us all things that pertain to life and godliness..." (2 Pet. 1:3). Paul tells us, "My God shall supply all your need according to His riches in glory by Christ Jesus" (Phil. 4:19), and "God has not given us a spirit of fear, but of power and of love and of a sound mind" (2 Tim. 1:7).

Questions to Consider

1. Parents, do you realize you are partners with God in parenting your children? Your children do not belong to you; they are on loan from God. Look up the following Scriptures and write them below, noting the role God plays in children's lives.

   Psalm 127:3 _____

   _____

   Isaiah 54:13 _____

   _____

   1 Samuel 2:21 _____

   _____

2. Christian parents, have you made a commitment for your home? Can you say with Joshua, "As for me and my house, we will serve the Lord" (Josh. 24:15)? If your answer is yes, what does your family think of this commitment? If your answer is no, consider taking this important step today.

3. Using a dictionary, look up the words *compromise* and *commitment*. Write the definitions below.

Compromise: _____

_____

Commitment: _____

_____

4. Ask yourself a tough question: "Am I guilty of compromising my commitment to Christ?" If you answered "Yes," ask the Lord for forgiveness and pledge today to renew your commitment to Him—in your workplace, church, and especially your home.

5. Contrast the following worldly notions regarding children and child-rearing with the Scriptures' admonitions. Look up each Scripture reference and write it below.

"Children have rights equal to those of their parents."
Colossians 3:20 _____

_____

_____

"Children should have complete freedom to develop their characters."
Proverbs 22:6 _____

_____

_____

"Children should never be spanked or punished; these things are degrading and will destroy their self-esteem."
Proverbs 13:24 _____

_____

_____

"Children should have the right to sue their parents for "forcing" certain spiritual and moral instruction upon them."
Deuteronomy 11:18-19 _____

_____

"Children should have complete sexual freedom."
2 Timothy 2:22 _____

_____

DISCIPLINE

The word *teach* means "to instruct, to guide, to cause to know." The word *train* means "to form by instruction, discipline, or drill." *Discipline* is defined as "to train or develop by instruction and exercise." Notice the difference? Teaching is about conveying; training is about shaping; discipline includes both. The Bible makes it clear parents are to both teach and train their children—that is, discipline them. Yet, like the word *obey,* discipline is a word unloved by both parents and children.

Parents, don't avoid discipline. First, set an example by being a disciplined parent. An unknown author said, "Children are natural mimics; they act like their parents in spite of every effort to teach them good manners." When parents lack discipline in their own lives, they are unable to discipline their children effectively. Second, discipline your children when they need it. If you refuse to discipline your children, you will ruin them: "…a child left to himself brings shame to his mother" (Prov. 29:15).

There are two kinds of discipline: corrective and preventive. For either to be effective, it must be meshed and reinforced with its counterpart.

Questions to Consider

1. Hundreds of books on parenting have been written and published. Yet God has given us the most effective parenting manual ever written: the Bible. How often do you read and study God's Word? _____

2. How frequently does Psalm 1:2 say we are to meditate on God's Word?

   ❑ Less than once weekly   ❑ 1 to 2 times weekly   ❑ Several times weekly
   ❑ Daily   ❑ 1 to 2 times daily   ❑ Several times daily

3. Consider the differences between corrective discipline and preventive discipline: Corrective discipline involves punishment for an offense. Preventive discipline involves positive and frequent interaction with your kids. What preventive discipline techniques are you currently using?

   ❑ I spend time with my kids—quantity as well as quality.

   ❑ I read to my kids on a regular basis.

   ❑ I play with my kids.

   ❑ I have family devotions that include my kids.

   ❑ Other: _____

4. The words *discipline* and *disciple* come from the same root word. In Matthew 28:19, what does Jesus tell us to do? _____

_____

Corrective Discipline

Tragically, our society has taught us to be scared of spanking our kids. We've cultivated a hands-off approach, fearing a spanking might damage their self-esteem. God's Word paints a very different picture of discipline than many of the misconceptions society tries to persuade us to believe.

God's Wisdom

First, the Bible clearly tells us children need discipline: "The rod and rebuke give wisdom, but a child left to himself brings shame to his mother" (Prov. 29:15). For parents committed to raising their children to be godly men and women, discipline is not an option. Without parents' attention and correction, children pursue paths that break their parents' hearts—and God's heart.

Perhaps most importantly, God tells us discipline is an expression of love, not abuse or uncontrolled anger. Interestingly, some parents are terrified that if they spank their child, the child will not love them. Nothing could be further from the truth. The Bible tells us: "For whom the LORD loves He corrects, just as a father the son in whom he delights" (Prov. 3:12). "He who spares his rod hates his son, but he who loves him disciplines him promptly" (Prov. 13:24). By correcting our children early, we steer them away from destructive paths that lead to far greater pain than parental discipline given in love.

We also learn from Scripture that discipline is most effective when a child is young. "Chasten your son while there is hope, and do not set your heart on his destruction" (Prov. 19:18). This verse also tells us the purpose of discipline is correction, not damage to, or destruction of, a child's spirit or body. Discipline is not about crushing a child's spirit; its purpose is to break self-will and enforce godly obedience.

Lastly, here's a fact about discipline that ought to get the attention of our results-oriented society: effective discipline produces positive results: "Foolishness is bound up in the heart of a child; the rod of correction will drive it far from him" (Prov. 22:15); "Do not withhold correction from a child, for if you beat him with a rod, he will not die. You shall beat him with a rod, and deliver his soul from hell" (Prov. 23:13-14); "Correct your son, and he will give you rest; yes, he will give delight to your soul" (Prov. 29:17).

While most of us agree "foolishness is bound up in the heart of a child," far fewer are willing to consistently carry out the second part: using the rod to drive the foolishness away. *Shebet*, the Hebrew word for *rod*, means "staff, branch, offshoot, club, sceptre, tribe."[48] In other words, a rod is something separate from the body. I believe if God wanted parents to discipline with hands or fists, He would have written that. Instead, while the Bible clearly tells parents to discipline with the rod, it never instructs parents to discipline with the hand.

Parents, use your hands for loving affirmation and correction, but use a rod or paddle—something that won't damage the child but will get his or her attention—as a method of discipline. Never strike a child in the face; that's brutality, not discipline, and it's clearly not biblical.

Skip's Tips

Here are a few tips on corrective discipline, some of which I'm still learning myself.

- **Don't use idle threats or bribes.** Rather, specifically instruct your children, warn them of the consequences of disobedience, and follow through. For example, tell them, "Don't do that. If you do, I'm going to spank you." If they don't obey, follow through—the first time, not the second or the third.

- **Don't discipline through criticism and comparison.** The phrase, "Why can't you be more like …?" can ruin a child. Love, appreciate, affirm, and discipline your children for who they are and what they do—not who they aren't and what they don't do.

- **Don't discipline your children when you're angry with them.** Heed the words of Henry Wadsworth Longfellow, who said, "Hard words bruise the heart of a child." Let them know you love them and make sure they know why they are being punished. You might tell them, "I've warned you and now I'm going to punish you. I still love you, but I have to punish you because disobeyed me." After disciplining, affirm your children by telling them you love them and by mentioning some of the positive qualities you appreciate about them.

- **Don't focus on the short-term effects of discipline.** Think of its long-range rewards. Don't structure or evaluate your discipline by the immature way they respond to you today. What matters more is the way they respond twenty years from now. By disciplining correctly now, you give both your children and yourself the gift of enabling them to look back and say, "Thank you. I love you. It worked."

- **Admit to your kids when you're wrong.** When you've messed up, tell them "I'm sorry." Children don't expect perfection, but they do expect, remember, and respect honesty. Trusting God with our children does not mean taking a backseat in their development. The New Testament tells us trust and faith are active, not passive. In fact, James tells us "faith without works is dead" (Jas. 2:26). So is parenting without involvement. With all of our might, we need to fight passivity. We need to be active and involved in our children's lives.

BUILDER'S NOTES

Parents, use your hands for loving affirmation and correction, but use a rod or paddle—something that won't damage the child but will get his or her attention—as a method of discipline.

BUILDER'S NOTES

Most important is not what your children think of you today, but what they will think of you twenty years from now.

Questions to Consider

1. What do the following Scriptures say about the manner in which God the Father disciplines His children?

Deuteronomy 8:5 _____

2 Samuel 7:14 _____

Hebrews 12:6-7 _____

Revelation 3:19 _____

2. Examine your disciplining techniques. Do you discipline your child effectively? What are your views on spanking? Have your views changed after reading this portion of the teaching in this manual, and if so, how?

_____

_____

3. How do your children view you at their particular stage of life?

_____

_____

4. If your children require continual discipline (most kids do), they may tell you, "I don't like you." However, most important is not what they think of you today, but what they will think of you twenty years from now. Based on your current relationship with them, which of the following do you think your children will say to you when they are grown?

❑ Thank you.

❑ I love you.

❑ You never spent any time with me.

❑ You listened to and cared about me.

❑ You never bothered to discipline me.

❑ You set boundaries and held me to them.

❑ Other:_____

Preventive Discipline

In addition to corrective discipline, what do today's families need to help their children excel? What can parents do to ensure their children grow up secure and loved, excelling in the things of God? A group of Harvard University sociologists performed an open-ended study (about 90 percent accurate) with the objective of identifying key factors that prevent children from becoming delinquent. In order, the top four key factors identified were:

1. A father's firm, fair, and consistent discipline.
2. A mother's supervision, and companionship during the day.
3. Parents who demonstrated affection toward one another and their children.
4. A family that spent time together participating in the same activity.[49]

Effective training takes time. When we train children, we're molding their character. Because no two children are alike, a parent's training must be individually tailored to each child. Different children have different temperaments and different pain thresholds. They have different needs that present themselves at different times and in different ways. In one of his plays, William Shakespeare wrote, "It is a wise father that knows his own child."[50]

Spending time as a family provides a great opportunity for parents—especially moms and dads who work during the week—to study their kids. Only through spending time with your children can you see what they react to, respond to, do well at, enjoy, and dislike.

Dr. Anthony P. Witham said, "Children spell love, T-I-M-E." Do you spend time with your kids? Do you read to them, love them, sing with them, play with them? If you don't, perhaps you have no right to spank them. By spending time with your children, loving them, and giving them the attention they crave, you can prevent many problems which result in the need for corrective discipline. Moreover, by practicing preventive discipline, you earn the right to reinforce it with corrective discipline.

In contrast, passive parenting almost ensures the development of insecurity and anger in our children. Parents, no matter what challenges you encounter, no matter how tired you become, I urge you not to withdraw, fall back, or give up. Trusting God with our children does not mean taking a backseat in their development. The New Testament tells us trust and faith are active, not passive. In fact, James tells us "...faith without works is dead..." (Jas. 2:26). So is parenting without involvement. With all of our might, we need to fight passivity. We need to be active and involved in our children's lives.

Tragic Statistics

Some recent national polls provide some tragic statistics. In a poll conducted by Public Agenda, a nonprofit research organization, 70 percent of parents said they had not volunteered to tutor or coach in the past two years, and 60 percent said they had not attended a single community event held at their child's school. In a U.S. Education Department survey conducted in 1999, 24 percent of kids felt their parents showed little or no interest in what they studied at school.[51]

Perhaps more than any other generation, today's families are guilty of not spending time together. American teens, in particular, are spending a growing amount of time outside the control of adults.[53] It's so easy to get out of touch and lose track of what's going on in each other's lives. Parents work long hours,

BUILDER'S NOTES

Dr. Anthony P. Witham said, "Children spell love, T-I-M-E." Do you spend time with your kids? Do you read to them, love them, sing with them, play with them? If you don't, perhaps you have no right to spank them.

attend business or social engagements, fit in visits to the health club, and only see their kids for more than two hours at a time on the weekends. Meanwhile, kids attend school, participate in sports or various activities after school, have homework or other activities in the evenings, and make plans with their friends on weekends.

Society tells us this type of lifestyle builds a well-rounded, multi-skilled family—the family of the new millennium. Empty hearts, broken lives, and statistics, however, tell a different story. Lack of time spent together by parents and children can lead to consequences that are disheartening at best and disastrous at worst. A well-known song written in 1974 conveys a poignant message to parents about the importance of time spent with their children.

BUILDER'S NOTES

In a Primedia/Roper National Youth Survey of three thousand teenagers, 47 percent ranked "lack of parental discipline of children and teens" among society's worst problems. How tragic!

A child arrived just the other day,
He came to the world in the usual way.
But there were planes to catch, and bills to pay.
He learned to walk while I was away.
And he was talking 'fore I knew it, and as he grew,
He'd say, "I'm gonna be like you, Dad.
You know I'm gonna be like you."

My son turned ten just the other day.
He said, "Thanks for the ball, Dad, come on let's play.
Can you teach me to throw?" I said, "Not today,
I got a lot to do." He said, "That's ok."
And he walked away, but his smile never dimmed,
Said, "I'm gonna be like him, yeah. You know I'm gonna be like him."

And the cat's in the cradle and the silver spoon,
Little boy blue and the man in the moon.
"When you coming home, Dad?" "I don't know when,
But we'll get together then. You know we'll have a good time then."

Well, he came from college just the other day,
So much like a man I just had to say,
"Son, I'm proud of you. Can you sit for a while?"
He shook his head, and he said with a smile,
"What I'd really like, Dad, is to borrow the car keys.
See you later. Can I have them please?"

And the cat's in the cradle and the silver spoon,
Little boy blue and the man in the moon.
"When you coming home, Son?" "I don't know when,
But we'll get together then, Dad. You know we'll have a good time then."

I've long since retired and my son's moved away.
I called him up just the other day.
I said, "I'd like to see you if you don't mind."
He said, "I'd love to, Dad, if I could find the time.
You see, my new job's a hassle, and the kid's got the flu,
But it's sure nice talking to you, Dad. It's been sure nice talking to you."
And as I hung up the phone, it occurred to me,
He'd grown up just like me. My boy was just like me.

And the cat's in the cradle and the silver spoon,
Little boy blue and the man in the moon.
"When you coming home, Son?" "I don't know when,
But we'll get together then, Dad. You know we'll have a good time then." [54]

Have you ever met a parent who regretted spending too much time with their kids? Have you ever heard a parent say, "I made a mistake! I spent too much time with my children and taught them too many spiritual things! Oh, I regret it"? I haven't. Too often I've heard great remorse expressed by parents who failed to spend adequate time with their children.

In the words of a *TIME* magazine article:

Parents who give up and back off leave their children at the mercy of a merciless culture. The ones who stand firm and stay involved often find their families grow closer, their kids stronger from being exposed to the toxins around them and building resistance to them. [55]

As inspiring as the previous song is grievous, the following is a different piece of prose written by a different parent. Called "A Letter to Jenna," it's a letter from author Max Lucado to his daughter.

Dearest Jenna,

I just put you to bed. Like every night, I rocked and you resisted. I sat in the chair with you and your pillow on my lap. You lay belly-down with arms spread. You turned your head from side to side, attempting to ward off the arriving slumber. But finally you surrendered; your legs stopped their twisting and your arms relaxed. Your body went limp, and your eyelids slid shut.

As you slept on my lap, I sat for awhile in the darkness. I stroked your golden curls and ran my fingers across your chubby cheeks. You were so still, so innocent, so full of life—even in your sleep.

I thought of tonight's big event. I couldn't get it off my mind. Tonight, for the first time, you walked! Oh, you'd taken little steps

 **BUILDER'S NOTES**

Too often I've heard great remorse expressed by parents who failed to spend adequate time with their children.

BUILDER'S NOTES

Life has a way of whispering to us when sacred moments are occurring. And life whispered tonight. As you released my hand and stepped alone, an emotion surged within me. An emotion that I didn't identify until I held you sleeping in my lap.

before, but always with caution and timidity. You would gingerly step one or two paces and then squat or fall. We had practiced with you many evenings. "Go to Mommy," I'd say and off you'd go, holding my hand until you could almost touch hers, then you'd solo for one or two, or even three steps and then tumble into her arms.

But tonight, tonight you were something to behold. Tonight you let go of my hand, spread your arms ever so slightly to get your balance, and you took off … 8, 9, 10, even 12 steps to Mommy. Then back you came. You turned your palms up, like you do when you want me to carry you, and started in my direction. You hesitated a few times. But then you got your courage and balance and came bounding to me. Oh, how we clapped and rejoiced!

Life has a way of whispering to us when sacred moments are occurring. And life whispered tonight. As you released my hand and stepped alone, an emotion surged within me. An emotion that I didn't identify until I held you sleeping in my lap.

What was I feeling? This may surprise you, but the emotion was fear. I was afraid. You see, Jenna, until tonight, you depended on your mother and me for everything. Everywhere you wanted to go, we took you. Anything you wanted to do, we did with you. But tonight marked, well, it marked your stepping out. Soon you won't want to be carried. Soon you will squirm from our arms to the floor and proudly walk alone.

I thought to myself, "If she had known what she was doing, would she have done it? Would she have taken that first step?"

Your first step away from childhood. Your first step away from innocence. Your first step away from home. Your first step away from us; away from our world and into your own.

I imagined, as I watched you sleep, other first steps that await us in the future.

I thought of your first step up the sidewalk to school. Freshly scrubbed with shiny shoes and pigtails braided by Mom, off you'll go into the big world of pencils, blackboards, and knowledge. Stepping proudly into the hallowed halls of chemistry, numbers, and words. What will you learn?
I wonder.

I thought of your first steps toward friendships. When "Christy" or "Megan" or who-knows-who next door knocks on our door and asks, "Can Jenna come and play?" When another little friend takes the place of Daddy as your buddy and Mom as your girlfriend. "Can I spend the night?"

And your first steps toward your own faith. God, I pray they come. One foot carefully, but doggedly, placed in front of the other carrying your heart to the Roman cross. Hands extended inviting God to lead you as you continue stepping through the unpredictable fields of faith and fear.

And your first step down the aisle. Your whiteness, your youth— your arm entwined in mine. Your hands full of flowers. Your heart full of hopes and promises. Down the aisle we'll step, you holding my hand as you did tonight. And then, releasing my hand as you did tonight. But this time taking, not the hand of your mother, but the hand of another. A young man to whom I will entrust the most precious treasure I've yet received: my little girl.

So, as I held you so quietly in the darkness, I felt fear. Fear that what we'd started tonight, we couldn't stop. I had a crazy yearning to push the "pause" button and freeze our days as they now are. You in our arms, forever giggling, kissing, and playing.

But life isn't like that. Those who love life must love it with open hands. We must release time and save only the memories. We must remember that with each first step comes a new journey of joy, surprises, and gentle whispers of God's presence.

So, I'll let you walk, little angel. I'll release your hand and let you go. And I'll do my best to stay nearby. And should you fall, I'll rush to help you up. And should you stumble, I'll catch you. And should your steps lead you astray, I'll do my best to show you the right path.

But Jenna, darling, I want you to know something. Should you ever grow weary of walking, or should you ever grow fearful of stepping into dark shadows, should you ever just need to stop and look to see if you're aimed in the right direction, I'm here. And, honey, you're never too old to do what you did tonight. You're never too old to curl up in my lap and sleep securely knowing that any evil, any pain, or even hell itself would have to deal with me before it could touch my precious Jenna.[56]

This child will grow up secure. She'll grow up loved. She'll grow up wanting to obey a father and mother who love her deeply, and who know the answer to parenting lies not in provoking, but in encouraging. This child will want to do the right thing because it's pleasing to the Lord and pleasing to her role model of the Lord: her daddy.

Questions to Consider

1. The Harvard University study identified factors that would enable children to grow up feeling secure and loved. How important are these four factors in your home?

Dad, is your discipline firm, fair, and consistent? _____

Mom, do you supervise and provide companionship to your kids? _____

Parents, do you demonstrate affection toward one another? _____

Do you demonstrate affection toward your children? _____

2. How often does your family spend time together, engaged in the same activity? _____

_____

3. Study your children and find out what is going on in their worlds. Read Prov. 22:6. What are parents told to do?

_____

_____

4. To train your children effectively, you need to know each child individually. On the lines below, write each child's name. Then check the characteristics in each list particular to that child. (If you have more than three children, copy and complete a list for each child on a separate sheet of paper. And God bless you!)

Child's Name	**Child's Name**	**Child's Name**
❏ Quiet	❏ Quiet	❏ Quiet
❏ Outspoken	❏ Outspoken	❏ Outspoken
❏ Sensitive	❏ Sensitive	❏ Sensitive
❏ Good sense of humor	❏ Good sense of humor	❏ Good sense of humor
❏ Gentle	❏ Gentle	❏ Gentle
❏ Rough and tumble	❏ Rough and tumble	❏ Rough and tumble
❏ Affectionate	❏ Affectionate	❏ Affectionate
❏ Prefers to be alone	❏ Prefers to be alone	❏ Prefers to be alone
❏ Prefers to be with others	❏ Prefers to be with others	❏ Prefers to be with others
❏ Active	❏ Active	❏ Active
❏ Sedate	❏ Sedate	❏ Sedate
❏ Other:_____	❏ Other:_____	❏ Other:_____
❏ Other:_____	❏ Other:_____	❏ Other:_____

BUILDER'S NOTES

To train your children effectively, you need to know each child individually.

5. The New Testament tells us faith is active, not passive. In like manner, we are to be involved parents who take an active role in our children's lives. What do the following Scriptures say about active faith?

Mark 5:34 _____

Luke 7:50 _____

Acts 6:8 _____

1 Corinthians 2:5 _____

1 Timothy 6:12 _____

James 2:26 _____

6. Mom and Dad, do you:

	Yes	No	Sometimes
Discuss your day with your kids?	❑	❑	❑
Ask your kids about their day and really listen to what they say?	❑	❑	❑
Praise your kids every day?	❑	❑	❑
Hug and kiss your kids frequently?	❑	❑	❑
Tell your kids you love them?	❑	❑	❑
Help your kids with their homework?	❑	❑	❑

7. Upon which item above will you commit to improve this week?

_____

BUILDER'S NOTES

What happens when parents become uninvolved in their children's lives? When parents fail to notice when their children need discipline, and thus fail to provide their children with the training God commands?

Passive Parenting

What happens when parents become uninvolved in their children's lives? When parents don't take time to understand their children's world and learn their children's likes and dislikes? When parents fail to notice when their children need discipline, and thus fail to provide their children with the training God commands? Genesis 37:12-36 shows us a family in which the parent detached from his children and what happened as a result. Sadly, this story is repeated thousands of times with every generation.

In this biblical example of a passive parent is Jacob (also called "Israel"), father of twelve sons. Although Jacob was outwardly familiar with his children, in many respects he didn't know them at all. He knew they were outwardly corrupt and violent, yet he was unaware of their inner feelings. Though Joseph's ten older brothers were responsible to God for their own criminal actions, we can see some definite problems with Jacob's parenting skills.

Self-Absorption

Scripture provides us with some background about Jacob's activities. From Genesis 30:43 we learn Jacob was fairly wealthy: "Thus the man became exceedingly prosperous, and had large flocks, female and male servants, and camels and donkeys." Later, when Jacob went back into the land of Canaan, he arrived at a place called Shechem. He liked Shechem so much that he settled there and bought a large portion of land there to raise his flocks. It appears Jacob passed his increasingly profitable business on to his ten sons who expanded the operation.

A terrible tragedy occurred while the family lived at Shechem. Jacob's only daughter, Dinah, was raped by a man named Shechem. Rather than abandoning her, Shechem fell in love with Dinah. "So Shechem spoke to his father Hamor, saying, 'Get me this young woman as a wife'" (Gen. 34:4).

We don't know Jacob's reaction to Hamor's request, but Genesis 34 tells us the reaction of Jacob's ten oldest sons. The brothers told Hamor, "We cannot do this thing, to give our sister to one who is uncircumcised, for that would be a reproach to us. But on this condition we will consent to you: If you will become as we are, if every male of you is circumcised, then we will give our daughters to you…" (Gen. 34:14-16). Shechem's family complied, with tragic results:

> Now it came to pass on the third day, when they were in pain, that two of the sons of Jacob, Simeon and Levi, Dinah's brothers, each took his sword and came boldly upon the city and killed all the males. And they killed Hamor and Shechem his son with the edge of the sword, and took Dinah from Shechem's house, and went out. The sons of Jacob came upon the slain, and plundered the city, because their sister had been defiled. They took their sheep, their oxen, and their donkeys, what was in the city and what was in the field, and all their wealth. All their little ones and their wives they took captive; and they plundered even all that was in the houses. Gen. 34:25-29

BUILDER'S NOTES

Notice Jacob uses "I" and "me" through his sentence. Jacob's response was that of a selfish, preoccupied father. He did not discipline his sons.

In verse 30 we see Jacob's response to the actions of his sons. He said to Simeon and Levi, "You have troubled me by making me obnoxious among the inhabitants of the land, among the Canaanites and the Perizzites; and since I am few in number, they will gather themselves together against me and kill me. I shall be destroyed, my household and I." Notice Jacob uses "I" and "me" through his sentence. Jacob's response was that of a selfish, preoccupied father. He did not discipline his sons. All he said was, "You really shouldn't have killed them. It made me look bad." He was concerned only about his own status.

Passing the Buck

Next, let's look at Genesis 35:

> *Then God said to Jacob, "Arise, go up to Bethel and dwell there; and make
> an altar there to God, who appeared to you when you fled from the face of
> Esau your brother." And Jacob said to his household and to all who were
> with him, "Put away the foreign gods that are among you, purify yourselves,
> and change your garments. Then let us arise and go up to Bethel; and I
> will make an altar there to God, who answered me in the day of my distress
> and has been with me in the way which I have gone."* Gen. 35:1-3

In response to God's command, Jacob tells his sons, in effect, "Kids, we're
going to church." I address this point because many parents deal with wayward
children this way. They say, "You kids are getting out of hand. You're going to
church! I can't raise you. The church will set you straight; that's their job." Will
it work? Let's do the math. If parents take their children to church weekly, the
children are in a ministry program approximately 52 hours each year. That
leaves children about 8,708 hours with their parents. If parents are unable to
correctly train their children in 8,708 hours, how likely is a church to correct
children's behavior in just 52?

I read an article called "The Biggest Mistakes Parents Make in Affecting
Teenagers." The author wrote:

> Parents make a big mistake when they don't start affecting their children
> in a favorable manner from day one. But they make a bigger, perhaps
> the biggest, mistake when they discover their dilemma late and become
> overly zealous to make up for lost time. A classic example is of two par-
> ents who attend a Family Life Conference. On the way home, they write
> twenty-five rules to post on the refrigerator with the corresponding pun-
> ishment for any infraction of the new regime. Upon arrival, they proud-
> ly announce, "As of today, we're going to…" and so on. It's no wonder
> that the fourteen and sixteen-year-old teenagers raise an eyebrow, heave a
> sigh, and think, "What have we gotten into?" Suddenly plung-
> ing in with a lot of new rules can really upset the apple cart. While a
> zealous attitude for reform is commendable, how you deliver the new
> policies is directly related to how well they will be received by your
> teens. When teens aren't so keen on the new rule system, parents often
> get discouraged and give up all together, not realizing that it was their
> manner that turned their kids off.[57]

Inaction

We find another important incident illustrated in Genesis 35:22: "Reuben went
and lay with Bilhah his father's concubine; and Israel heard about it." Scripture
provides no evidence Jacob did anything in response; he just heard about it.

BUILDER'S NOTES

*When teens aren't so
keen on the new rule
system, parents often get
discouraged and give up
all together, not
realizing that it was
their manner that
turned their kids off.*

Similarly, when Dinah was raped, all we're told is that Jacob heard about it. Inaction seems to be his consistent mode of operation.

Ignorance

All this brings us to Genesis 37, where Jacob sends Joseph to his ten sons in Shechem. In Genesis 37:14, Jacob said to Joseph, "[P]lease go and see if it is well with your brothers and well with the flocks, and bring back word to me." Why? Think about all we just read. Jacob was probably wondering what kind of trouble his sons might be getting into in Shechem, and consequently, how their behavior might be affecting his investment.

Jacob was well aware of his sons' corrupt tendencies. However, he seemingly failed to see the depth of their envy and hatred of Joseph. Scripture tells us, "Now Israel loved Joseph more than all his children, because he was the son of his old age. Also he made him a tunic of many colors. But when his brothers saw that their father loved him more than all his brothers, they hated him and could not speak peaceably to him…They hated him even more for his dreams and for his words" (Gen. 37:3-4, 8). Had Jacob been more observant of his sons, he would have been aware of the danger in which he was placing Joseph. In turn, he likely would not have sent his favored son alone on a mission to "see if it is well with your brothers."

A Lamentable Legacy

Jacob was a passive and preoccupied father. He neglected to discipline his sons and be effectively involved in their lives. How did this affect his sons' development? Let's look at their response to Joseph's arrival: "Now when they saw him afar off, even before he came near them, they conspired against him to kill him" (Gen. 37:18).

The brothers look off in the horizon. The sun is just right and they see a figure coming toward them. "Hey, who's that?" one brother asks. "I don't know," responds another, "but the walk looks familiar." Another brother replies, "Oh, I know who that is! Look at that robe shining in the sun. That's Joseph." I can just hear them saying, "Remember when he tattled on us?" (see Gen. 37:2). "Yeah, I hated him for that and I've never forgiven him." "Remember those stupid dreams he had, about how we're going to bow to him?" (see Gen. 37:5-11). Even before Joseph reached his brothers, they began plotting to harm him:

> *"Come therefore, let us now kill him and cast him into some pit; and we shall say, 'Some wild beast has devoured him.' We shall see what will become of his dreams!" But Reuben heard it, and he delivered him out of their hands, and said, "Let us not kill him." And Reuben said to them, "Shed no blood, but cast him into this pit which is in the wilderness, and do not lay a*

BUILDER'S NOTES

Jacob was a passive and preoccupied father. He neglected to discipline his sons and be effectively involved in their lives.

hand on him"—that he might deliver him out of their hands, and bring him back to his father. So it came to pass, when Joseph had come to his brothers, that they stripped Joseph of his tunic, the tunic of many colors that was on him. Then they took him and cast him into a pit. And the pit was empty; there was no water in it. And they sat down to eat a meal. Then they lifted their eyes and looked, and there was a company of Ishmaelites, coming from Gilead with their camels, bearing spices, balm, and myrrh, on their way to carry them down to Egypt. So Judah said to his brothers, "What profit is there if we kill our brother and conceal his blood? Come and let us sell him to the Ishmaelites, and let not our hand be upon him, for he is our brother and our flesh." And his brothers listened. Then Midianite traders passed by; so the brothers pulled Joseph up and lifted him out of the pit, and sold him to the Ishmaelites for twenty shekels of silver. And they took Joseph to Egypt. Gen. 37:20-28

BUILDER'S NOTES

Joseph's other brothers were self-centered as well. Note Judah's question, "What profit is there if we kill our brother" (Gen. 37:26)?

Some view Reuben's interruption of his brothers' plot as heroic. They think, "Good. Reuben, the firstborn, is stepping in." I'm not so sure Reuben's intentions were pure. When Judah proposes selling Joseph to the Ishmaelites, Scripture records no protest from Reuben. He also quickly agrees to the cover-up story that a wild beast attacked and ate Joseph.

Let's remember a few things about Reuben. Reuben was the firstborn son, but Scripture tells us Jacob "…loved Joseph more than all his children…" (Gen. 37:3). Reuben hated Joseph for that. Also, Reuben committed incest with one of Jacob's concubines. As Reuben spoke up in favor of sparing Joseph's life, I suspect he was thinking, "Maybe there's a way here to recover myself and my position. If I deliver Joseph unharmed to my father, perhaps my position won't be permanently given to Joseph, and I'll be off the hook for sleeping with my father's concubine."

Notice Reuben's words after Joseph had been sold to the Midianites: "Then Reuben returned to the pit, and indeed Joseph was not in the pit; and he tore his clothes. And he returned to his brothers and said, 'The lad is no more; and I, where shall I go?'" (Gen. 37:29-30). Again, we see the word "I," just as Jacob used it in Genesis 34:30. Reuben's concern was solely for his own welfare, not Joseph's or Jacob's. I'm sure he thought, "It was my idea to throw him into the pit. I'm the firstborn. I'm already in trouble. I could be hung on this one! Where am I going to go?"

Joseph's other brothers were self-centered as well. Note Judah's question, "What profit is there if we kill our brother?" (Gen. 37:26). In other words, "Hey, this doesn't make sense! Why kill Joseph when we can make money by selling him?" That's the legacy of Jacob. He was a deceiver and conniver who did many things solely for financial gain (see Gen. 27:6-29; 30:32-43).

As we look at the life of Jacob, we see a man who lacked real care and concern for his children. Sadly, but not surprisingly, that pattern was repeated in his own children. They turned out just like dad: insensitive, unfeeling, and uncaring about relationships. The story ends:

> *So they took Joseph's tunic, killed a kid of the goats, and dipped the tunic in the blood. Then they sent the tunic of many colors, and they brought it to their father and said, "We have found this. Do you know whether it is your son's tunic or not?" And he recognized it and said, "It is my son's tunic. A wild beast has devoured him. Without doubt Joseph is torn to pieces." Then Jacob tore his clothes, put sackcloth on his waist, and mourned for his son many days. And all his sons and all his daughters arose to comfort him; but he refused to be comforted, and he said, "For I shall go down into the grave to my son in mourning." Thus his father wept for him.* Gen. 37:31-35

This was a sad day for Jacob. Ten of his sons had turned out just like him, and the son he loved most had just become a memory.

Questions to Consider

1. Ask yourself this important question: Am I guilty of being a passive parent?

   ❏ Sometimes   ❏ Occasionally   ❏ Never

2. Jacob knew his sons were outwardly corrupt and violent (Gen. 34:7-29), but he failed to be aware of their animosity toward Joseph. Read Genesis 37:3-10. What in this passage indicates that Jacob should have had an inkling of the existing sibling rivalry?

   _____

   _____

3. In the following passage, highlight, or underline each use by Jacob of the words *I* or *me*.

   > *Then Jacob said to Simeon and Levi, "You have troubled me by making me obnoxious among the inhabitants of the land, among the Canaanites and the Perizzites; and since I am few in number, they will gather themselves together against me and kill me. I shall be destroyed, my household and I."* Genesis 34:30

4. With whom was Jacob most concerned in the passage above?

   ❏ Dinah   ❏ Joseph   ❏ His ten older sons   ❏ Himself

5. Many parents expect their church's children's ministry to help raise their children. Examine your hearts, Mom and Dad. What is the primary reason you bring your kids to Sunday school?

   ❏ So they can get the discipline they need.

❑ So I can have a couple of hours of peace and quiet.

❑ So they can learn more about God and Jesus and fellowship with other believers.

❑ Other: _____

6. At least twice Jacob "heard" what his sons had done, but failed to do anything about their behavior. How do you discipline your children? When you hear they have misbehaved, do you ignore their behavior, make light of it, or address it with godly discipline? _____

_____

7. If you have become a passive parent, confess it to the Lord. Ask Him to help you "put off" your passivity and "put on" a renewed, active interest in your children.

A FINAL WORD

Parents, don't be passive. Know your children. Discipline your children. Love your children with your life. God places this responsibility squarely on your shoulders. Whether you accept it or not, God holds you responsible for the training your child receives or doesn't receive. You could place your faith in Sunday schools and Christian schools to train your children in the way they should go, but what if they fail? God will hold you responsible. Every parent's job is to bring his or her children up in the nurturing and admonition of the Lord.

Finally, be encouraged. Learn from mistakes—both others' and your own—so you don't repeat them. But don't dwell on regrets and weigh yourself down with guilt. As I said at the beginning of this chapter, there's no such thing as a "perfect parent." Let the life of Joseph reassure you: You can make a lot of mistakes, yet still have a child turn out as well as Joseph.

I'll close with a story I once heard a man tell about his childhood:

> When I was about thirteen years old, my little brother was about ten. One Saturday morning, as the family was gathered around the table, Dad said, "I'm taking you to the circus this afternoon." We were all excited. About noon we sat down for lunch and the telephone rang. My dad picked it up and I knew trouble was brewing. Something had come up at the office downtown that demanded his attention right away. We were sure our father was going to have to go to work and were bracing ourselves for the disappointment, when we heard Dad say, "I know it's important, but it's going to have to wait." He hung up the phone and went back to the lunch table. My mom turned to my dad, put her hand lovingly upon his arm and said, "Honey, it's all right, the circus keeps

🏠 **BUILDER'S NOTES**

Learn from mistakes—both others' and your own—so you don't repeat them.

coming back to town." He said, "I know it does, but childhood doesn't." My father's decision to cancel something was very important for us.

That father made a sacrificial decision to be actively involved in his children's lives. Can you imagine how that father's decision made his children feel? They knew they were their father's most important agenda.

Question to Consider

Write a prayer to the Father, asking Him for direction, strength and wisdom to become and remain a parent after His own heart, who will do His will (Acts 13:22).

_____

_____

_____

_____

_____

_____

_____

_____

_____

_____

_____

_____

_____

Endnotes

REFERENCES

[1] Rick Lyman, "Family Films are Hollywood's Hot Tickets," *New York Times*, Mar. 7, 2000.

[2] Joseph Pereira, "Focus on Family Time Becomes Boon for Makers of Board Games," *Wall Street Journal*, Dec. 14, 2000, p. B16.

[3] Shelly Branch, "100 Best Companies to Work for in America," *Fortune*, Jan. 11, 1999, Vol. 139, Issue 1, p. 118.

[4] Veronica Chambers, "Family Rappers," *Newsweek*, Jan. 19, 1998, Vol. 131, Issue 3, p. 66.

[5] David Graham Cooper, *The Death of the Family*, New York, Pantheon Books, 1971.

[6] Ron Klinger, "What Can Be Done About Absentee Fathers?" *USA Today Magazine*, July 1998, Vol. 127, Issue 2638, p. 30.

[7] "Most Important Problem," The Gallup Organization, Oct. 2000.

[8] George Roche, "Is the U.S. Morally in Trouble?" *USA Today Magazine*, Jan. 1997, Vol. 125, Issue 2660, p.26.

[9] Marianne M. Jennings, What's Behind the Growing Generation Gap?" *USA Today Magazine*, Nov. 1999, Vol. 128, Issue 2654, p. 14.

[10] George Roche, "Is the U.S. morally in trouble?" *USA Today Magazine*, Jan. 1997, Vol. 125, Issue 2660, p. 26.

[11] James Dobson, *Straight Talk to Men,* Word Publishers, ©1995, p. 120.

[12] See Genesis 2:15-24.

[13] Marianne M. Jennings, "What's Behind the Growing Generation Gap?" *USA Today Magazine*, Nov. 1999, Vol. 128, Issue 2654, p14.

[14] See Merrill F. Unger, R.K. Harrison (Editor), *The New Unger's Bible Dictionary*, Moody Press, Apr. 1999.

[15] Steve Farrar, *Point Man,* ©1990, Multnomah, p. 21.

[16] Barclay, William Daily Study Bible Series: *The Letters to the Philippians, Colossians and Thessalonians* (Revised Edition), Westminster John Knox Press, ©1975.

[17] James Dobson, *Straight Talk to Men and Their Wives,* Word Inc., ©1980, p. 14–15.

[18] Chuck Swindoll, *Think it Over: Love Without a Net,* a publication of the First Evangelical Free Church of California.

[19] Albert Barnes, *Barnes' Notes on the New Testament*, Kregel Publications.

[20] Richard Selzer M.D., *Mortal Lessons: Notes on the Art of Surgery,* Simon & Schuster, ©1978, p. 45–46.

[21] Tamala M. Edwards, Tammerlin Drummond, Elizabeth Kaufman, Anne Moffett, Jacqueline Savaiano
, Maggie Sieger, "Flying Solo," *TIME Canada*, August 28, 2000, Vol. 156, Issue 9, p. 36.

[22] Kate Millett, *Sexual Politics*, Doubleday, ©1970.

[23] *Webster's Revised Unabridged Dictionary*, MICRA, Inc., ©1996, 1998.

[24] *Roget's II: The New Thesaurus, Third Edition*, Houghton Mifflin Company, ©1995.

[25] *Webster's Revised Unabridged Dictionary*, MICRA, Inc., ©1996, 1998.

[26] *Roget's II: The New Thesaurus, Third Edition*, Houghton Mifflin Company, ©1995.

[27] Source unknown.

[28] Thayer and Smith, *The KJV New Testament Greek Lexicon.*

[29] Dennis Rainey, *Staying Close*, Word Publishing, ©1992.

[30] Ibid.

[31] The Bible: *James Moffat Translation,* Harper & Row Pulishers, Inc., ©1954, p. 732.

[32] Linda Davis, *How to be the Happy Wife of an Unsaved Husband*, Whitaker House, ©1986.

[33] See Acts 9:36-42.

[34] See Ephesians 5:25-28, 33.

[35] *The Brown-Driver-Briggs Hebrew and English Lexicon*, Hendrickson Publishers, ©1996.

[36] See Ex. 20:12; Deut. 5:16; Matt. 15:4; Matt. 19:18; Mark 7:10; Mark 10:19; Luke 18:20; Eph. 6:2.

[37] James Dobson, *Straight Talk to Men,* Word Publishing, ©1995, p. 122.

[38] Ibid., p. 123.

[39] "When the Rehabilitation Ideal Fails: A Study of Parental Rights Termination," *Child Welfare*, July/Aug. 2001, Vol. 80, Issue 4, p. 405–432.

[40] Augustine, *Confessions*, Book Two, Chapter III, 5.

[41] James S. Hewett, *Illustrations Unlimited,* Tyndale House Publishers, Inc., ©1988, p. 376.

[42] Lydia Saad, "Mothers Get Winning Ratings in Gallup Poll," *Gallup News Service*, May 12, 2000.

[43] Ibid.

[44] "They Call Her Mother," author and original source unknown.

[45] *Nelson's Illustrated Bible Dictionary*, Thomas Nelson Publishers, ©1986.

[46] *The Brown-Driver-Briggs Hebrew and English Lexicon*, Hendrickson Publishers, ©1996.

[47] Rex R. Burns, *Pulpit Helps,* Chatanooga, TN.

[48] *The Brown-Driver-Briggs Hebrew and English Lexicon*, Hendrickson Publishers, ©1996.

[49] John MacArthur, *The Family*, Moody Press, ©1982, p. 100.

[50] William Shakespeare, *The Merchant of Venice*, Act 2, Scene 2.

[51] Jodie Morse, "When Parents Drop Out," *TIME*, May 21, 2001, Vol. 157, Issue 20, p. 80–83.

[52] Booth Moore, "News, Trends, Gossip and Stuff To Do; Here and Now; The Trouble With Adults Today," *The Los Angeles Times,* Jan. 20, 1999.

[53] Frank Furstenburg, "The sociology of adolescence and youth in the 1990s: A critical commentary," *Journal of Marriage and the Family*, Nov. 2000.

[54] Sandra Chapin, "Cat's in the Cradle," *Verities & Balderdash*, Elektra, ©1974.

[55] Nancy Gibbs, Tim Padgett, "Who's in Charge Here?" *TIME*, Aug. 6, 2001, Vol. 158, Issue 5, p. 40–49.

[56] Max Lucado, "A Letter to Jenna," UpWords Ministries, ©1990. Used by permission.

[57] Jay Kesler, Gen. Editor, *Parents and Teenagers*, Victor Books, ©1985, p. 40.